25 WALKS

HIGHLAND
PERTHSHIRE

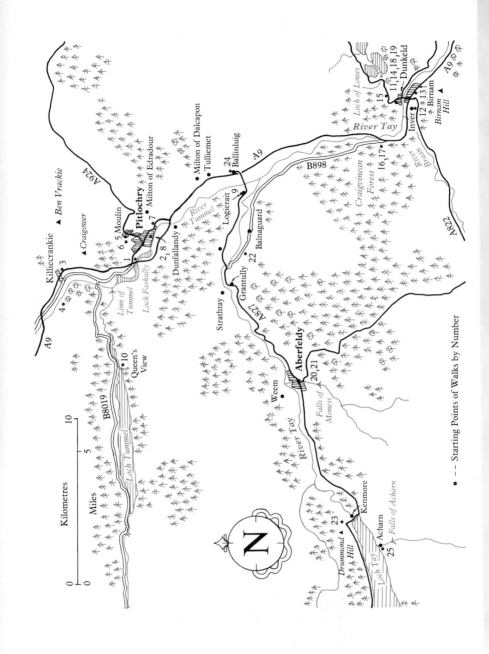

Ben Vrackie ▲

Craigower ▲

A924

Killiecrankie

Linn of Tummel

Loch Faskally

3

4

Queen's View

10

B8019

Loch Tummel

6 5 Moulin

Pitlochry

1   2, 8

Dunfallandy

7

River Tummel

Logierait

9

Strathtay

Grantully

Balnaguard

22

A827

Weem

Aberfeldy

20, 21

Falls of Moness

River Tay

Drummond Hill ▲

23

Kenmore

Loch Tay

Acharn

25

Falls of Acharn

Milton of Edradour

Milton of Dalcapon

Tulliemet

Ballinluig

Tummel

24

A9

B898

Craigvinean Forest

16, 17

River Tay

Loch of Lowes

15

Dunkeld

11, 14, 18, 19

Inver

12 13

Birnam

Birnam Hill ▲

River Braan

A9

A822

— — Starting Points of Walks by Number

Kilometres

Miles

10

5

0

0

N

25 WALKS

HIGHLAND PERTHSHIRE

Roger Smith

Series Editor: Roger Smith

SCOTTISH ENTERPRISE TAYSIDE

EDINBURGH:HMSO

Applications for reproduction should be made to HMSO

Acknowledgements

A number of people have helped greatly with the compilation of this book. I would especially like to thank John Dunn, Senior Countryside Ranger with Perth & Kinross District Council, for very helpful advice. The District Council have done great things in opening up and extending the network of walks available in the area.

I would also like to thank Chris Ford and Syd House of Forest Enterprise; Andrew Gordon, Factor for the Atholl Estates; Stakis Hotels; Ian Reynolds of Scottish Enterprise Tayside for financial support; and HMSO Scotland for giving me the job in the first place and for continued encouragement and support.

The Publishers thanks are due to the following: Scottish Enterprise Tayside; The National Trust for Scotland; The Forestry Commission; Historic Scotland and The Scottish Wildlife Trust for access to and use of transparencies throughout the book.

British Library Cataloguing in Publication Data

A catalogue record for this book is available from the British Library

Cover illustration: Faskally House and Craigower Hill.

ISBN 0 11 495168 3

CONTENTS

USEFUL INFORMATION

The length of each walk is given in kilometres and miles, but within the text measurements are metric for simplicity. The walks are described in detail and are supported by accompanying maps (study them before you start the walk), so there is little likelihood of getting lost, but if you want a back-up you will find the 1:25 000 Pathfinder Ordnance Survey maps on sale locally.

Every care has been taken to make the descriptions and maps as accurate as possible, but the author and publishers can accept no responsibility for errors, however caused. The countryside is always changing and there will inevitably be alterations to some aspects of these walks as time goes by. The publishers and author would be happy to receive comments and suggested alterations for future editions of the book.

Abbreviations
A number of abbreviations are used within the text. Usually these are explained, but a few, used frequently, are explained here.

NTS: The National Trust for Scotland. NTS has in its care over 100 properties of all kinds, ranging from small vernacular cottages and individual landscape features to great houses and large areas of superb mountain country.

OS: Ordnance Survey. The OS is our national mapping agency, covering the whole of the UK at various scales. The two scales most frequently used by walkers are 1:25 000 and 1:500 000. All OS maps are drawn on a grid of kilometre squares.

RSPB: Royal Society for the Protection of Birds. The largest conservation body of its kind in the UK with a membership approaching one million.

SNH: Scottish Natural Heritage. The government's conservation agency in Scotland. Formed in 1992 by a merger of the former Nature Conservancy Council and the Countryside Commission for Scotland, SNH has a remit covering scientific research, habitat conservation, access and recreation.

METRIC MEASUREMENTS

At the beginning of each walk, the distance is given in miles and kilometres. Within the text, all measurements are metric for simplicity (and indeed our Ordnance Survey maps are now all metric). However, it was felt that a conversion table might be useful to those readers who, like the author, still tend to think in Imperial terms.

The basic statistic to remember is that one kilometre is five-eighths of a mile. Half a mile is equivalent to 800 metres and a quarter-mile is 400 metres. Below that distance, yards and metres are little different in practical terms.

km	miles
1	0.625
1.6	1
2	1.25
3	1.875
3.2	2
4	2.5
4.8	3
5	3.125
6	3.75
6.4	4
7	4.375
8	5
9	5.625
10	6.25
16	10

INTRODUCTION

This book describes 25 walks in a roughly triangular area with Killiecrankie, Kenmore and Dunkeld as its three corners. It is an area rightly famed for its varied and beautiful scenery, and also has many fascinating historical connections. The walks visit ancient stone circles and burial mounds, mysterious Pictish stones, historic castles, a major battle site and many other equally interesting places. The wildlife is also rich.

In compiling the book, I have tried to keep in mind the visitor who enjoys a walk rather than the hardened hillwalker who wishes to bag half a dozen tops in a day. Most of the walks are between four and eight miles in length, and are well within the compass of any reasonably fit person. Most are very suitable for children, being on good paths and tracks. There is one genuine hillwalk (Ben Vrackie), on a well-used path that leads to a summit with a superb panoramic view. Try to keep a good day aside for that one if you can.

The weather in this part of Scotland is inevitably variable, but Perthshire (and the east generally) is drier than the west, and you will be very unlucky not to have some sunshine during your stay. April to June are often the driest months, with July and August rather damper. However, there are compensations for that as several of the walks visit very fine waterfalls which are at their best after periods of rain.

Generally speaking, sophisticated protective clothing should not be needed apart from the hillwalk mentioned above, when it is essential to carry good waterproofs. Information at the beginning of each walk indicates whether strong footwear such as boots is advised: in most cases the walks can be completed in trainers without any difficulty.

The length of each walk is given in kilometres and miles, but within the text, measurements are metric for simplicity. The walk descriptions, and the accompanying maps, should be sufficiently detailed to avoid the possibility of getting lost; many of the walks are waymarked too. However, if you like a back-up then I recommend the 1:25 000 Pathfinder Ordnance Survey maps, which are on sale locally.

The walks should all be suitable for families, and most can easily be completed by all but the very youngest children. If you take a dog, please ensure that it is kept under close control. Dogs should be kept on a lead when crossing farmland, and during the lambing period (March to May in this part of Scotland) you are asked not to take dogs through fields of sheep.

If you complete all these walks, you will have got to know the area and its delights quite well. I hope those you do complete will be enjoyable and will whet your appetite for further visits and perhaps longer excursions. Even though I am fortunate enough to live in the area, I never tire of exploring it on foot – by far the best way – and I am always coming across new views, hidden corners and previously undiscovered historical connections.

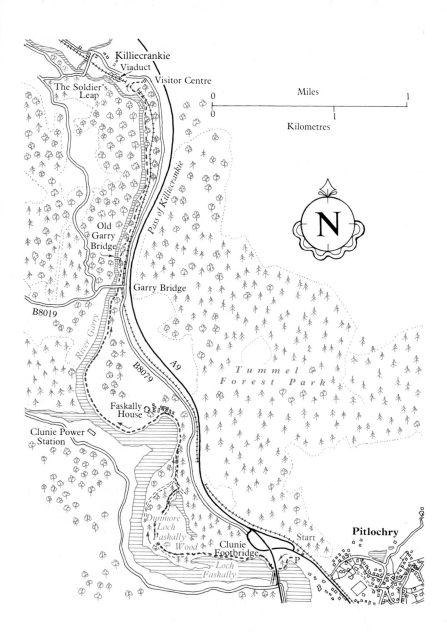

THE PASS OF KILLIECRANKIE

Killiecrankie is famous for the 1689 battle but the gorge is also a superb natural site with a fine river, lovely trees and a good range of wildlife. This out-and-back walk provides a pleasant, straightforward introduction to the area.

From the car park, where there is a small café and shop, and where boats can be hired, follow the signposts and walk beside Loch Faskally to pass under the bridge carrying the A9. The bridge, constructed by Balfour Beatty, won a Saltire Society award for its design. Beside it is the Clunie footbridge, which formerly carried a minor road. Loch Faskally was artificially created as part of a major hydro-electric scheme but now appears as a natural part of the scene.

INFORMATION

Distance: 8 km (5 miles).

Start and finish: Clunie car park, reached by taking the B8019 road from Pitlochry and turning off 2 km north of the town following Tay Forest Park signs.

Terrain: Good tracks and paths. No special footwear needed.

Refreshments: Café at start, and at the National Trust for Scotland Visitor Centre at Killiecrankie (both open April–October). Toilets at the Visitor Centre.

Opening hours NTS Visitor Centre at Killiecrankie: 1 Apr–31 Oct daily, 0930–1800 Jun–Aug, otherwise 1000–1700. Admission charge for non-members. Rangers regularly lead walks – details at the Centre or from the tourist information centre in Pitlochry.

Glorious autumn colours in the Pass.

Continue into Faskally Wood by a zigzag path up steps, following white markers on posts. The path winds through the wood, which has a good variety of trees and is often rich in birdsong, with the traffic noise from the A9 gradually diminishing as you walk. After about 1 km the path goes downhill to pass the very attractive Dunmore Loch, reedy, busy with waterfowl and fringed by rhododendrons, a riot of colour in season.

Dunmore Loch.

Past the loch, turn left on a minor road which leads to the Freshwater Biological Research Station. Before reaching the laboratories, turn left following a signpost to walk back to the lochside around the grounds of Faskally House, for many years used as an outdoor centre by Strathclyde Regional Council but with some doubts as to its future at the time this book was written.

The walk now continues beside the River Garry as it empties into the loch, with the Clunie Power Station opposite. The Garry is a spate river, and in flood rises very rapidly. When it is low, extensive shingle banks are revealed. The Pass of Killiecrankie is now clearly visible ahead, and in the distance, half right, is the bulk of Carn Liath ('the grey hill', and well named).

At the end of the fields, turn right (yellow arrow) then left down steps to cross a burn. Pass under the Garry Bridge, which carries the B8019 high overhead, and walk into the gorge, passing an old milestone which tells that you are 11 miles from Tummel Bridge and 3 from Blair Atholl. This is a very old route through the gorge, and was the only way through until the railway and the successive modern roads were made. The latest of these is high above to the right, on a viaduct as it cuts directly across the hillslope.

The path passes the old Garry Bridge, now a footbridge, and then reaches the Balfour Stone, where Brigadier Barthold Balfour of the Dutch Brigade, commander of the left wing of General Mackay's army, was killed in the 1689 battle. The full story of the battle is told at the National Trust for Scotland's excellent Visitor Centre, towards which you are now heading. The Centre was extended in 1993 and has displays on the wildlife and geology of the area as well as on the battle.

In summary, the battle, between government forces under Mackay and Jacobite rebels under John Graham of Claverhouse, more popularly known as 'Bonnie Dundee', did not take place in the gorge but at a place known as *Raon Ruiridh* (Rory's Field) about a mile to the north. Dundee felt he could gain an advantage here as Mackay's troops, horses and waggons struggled through the narrow pass. The battle, on the evening of 27 July 1689, was short and decisive, the Jacobites routing the government army in a matter of minutes. Many fleeing men were killed in the pass as they tried to escape. Dundee himself, who insisted on leading his men, was also killed, and without his inspirational leadership the rebellion fizzled out over the following months. Rob Roy MacGregor and his father Donald were among the Jacobite force on that July day.

Actors in period dress re-enact scenes from the 1689 Battle at the Visitor Centre.

The scene today is entirely peaceful as the path continues beside the river, passing John Mitchell's fine railway viaduct and then leading up steps to the site of the Soldier's Leap, where an escapee, Donald MacBean, is said to have jumped the gorge – not a leap that many would fancy, but it is surprising what you can achieve when desperation calls and your life is threatened.

The path continues upwards to reach the Visitor Centre at the roadside. After visiting the Centre, the return is made by the same route, which is no hardship. This is a lovely walk at any time of year, but as with many walks in this area, it is perhaps particularly fine in the autumn, when the colouring on the trees is quite spectacular.

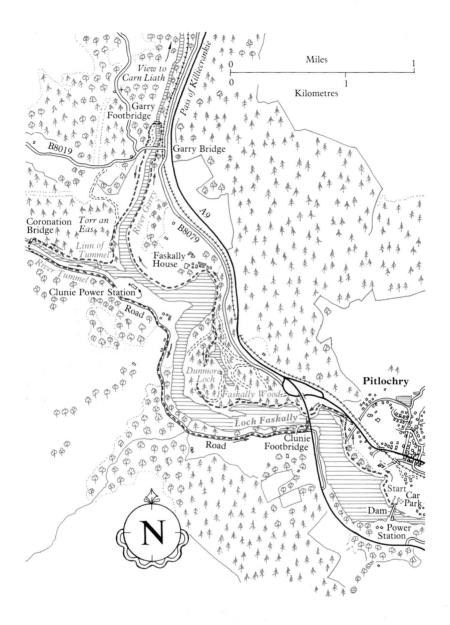

Miles

0   1

0   1

Kilometres

View to Carn Liath

Garry Footbridge

Garry Bridge

B8019

Pass of Killiecrankie

River Garry

A9

B8079

Coronation Bridge

Torr an Eas

Linn of Tummel

River Tummel

Faskally House

Clunie Power Station

Road

Dunmore Loch

Faskally Wood

Pitlochry

Loch Faskally

Road

Clunie Footbridge

Start

Car Park

Dam

Power Station

N

AROUND LOCH FASKALLY

This walk, one of the longer outings in the book, makes a 'grand tour' of Loch Faskally and its surroundings and offers a variety of scene that is satisfying at any time of the year. The trees are at their best in spring, when the fresh green leaf is vivid, and in autumn, when the colours are majestic against the backdrop of loch and mountain.

From the dam car park, walk down to the loch and turn right, following the signpost marked Killiecrankie. When the path forks stay left, by the loch. Faskally is an artificial loch created for a hydro-electric scheme in the 1950s but is none the less attractive for that. After a further 600 m go right beside a high wooden fence and then a stone wall. Turn left at the road and walk past Green Park Hotel to reach the Clunie car park (seasonal shop and café).

INFORMATION

Distance: 13 km (8 miles).

Start and finish: Pitlochry dam car park, signposted from the town centre.

Terrain: Roads, tracks and paths. No special footwear needed.

Refreshments: Wide selection in Pitlochry. Seasonal café at Clunie car park.

Opening hours Pitlochry power station and dam: Apr–Oct, daily 1000–1730, free (charge for exhibition). Fish ladder, exhibition on hydro-electric power, videos.

Looking down on Loch Faskally in autumn.

From here the walk follows the same outward path as walk 1 until the Garry footbridge. Turn left as signposted and walk under the A9 bridge crossing the loch, with the Clunie footbridge beside it, somewhat dwarfed by the newer construction. Continue into Faskally Wood by a zigzag path up steps and walk through the wood, following white marker posts. There is an attractive mixture of trees and generally a good range of birdlife to be heard, if not seen.

Dunmore Loch.

The path winds through the wood for about 1 km and then drops down beside the pretty little Dunmore Loch, the scene brightened further in spring by a fine display of rhododendrons. Past the loch, turn left onto a road and just before reaching the Freshwater Biological Laboratory, turn left off the road to rejoin the lochside walk around the perimeter fence of Faskally House.

Continue, now beside the River Garry, into the Pass of Killiecrankie. The name comes from the Gaelic 'coille chreithnich' meaning 'wood of shivering trees (possibly aspens)'. The pass is still attractively wooded with many fine broadleaved trees. Pass under the new Garry Bridge carrying the B8019 road and a little further on, cross the river by the footbridge. Looking north up the pass there is a superb view of the gorge and, framed in its steep sides, Carn Liath ('grey hill'), one of the Beinn y Ghlo group of hills beyond Blair Atholl.

Turn left across the bridge and walk back under the road bridge; you are actually on an old road here. The path then passes between the river and a large hayfield from which a crop is still taken each year. Across the field is the heavily wooded Torr an Eas ('waterfall hill'). The path climbs some steps and curves away from the Garry to reach the River Tummel, the other main feeder into Loch Faskally, at Linn of Tummel. A small plaque right down by the water here records a visit by Queen Victoria. The Linn was given to the National Trust for Scotland in 1944 by Dr Barbour of Bonskeid.

Linn means 'pool' and Tummel is tun allt, 'a plunging stream', but at the time of the Queen's visit this spot was known as the Falls of Tummel. There are still attractive small waterfalls but they were higher and more impressive before the hydro-electric scheme altered the

A boathouse sits beside the tranquil loch.

river flow. On the right here is a cutting in the rock: this was a salmon pass, built so that fish could bypass the falls. Continue by the Tummel, the path winding around in the trees, for nearly 1 km to reach the pretty Coronation Bridge. Cross it and walk up to the road.

Turn left and walk along this road, which is followed for 4 km above the western shore of Loch Faskally. The road carries little traffic and there are many fine views across the loch and to the east over the town to Ben Vrackie. On the way, the Clunie Power Station is passed. Beside it is a car park and picnic area which is popular with weekend visitors, and above it on the road is the Clunie Arch, built both to mark the opening of the power station and also in memory of five men who sadly lost their lives during the construction of the hydro-electric scheme.

The road curves east, looking across the loch at Faskally Wood, through which you walked earlier, and ahead to the two bridges which span the loch. One carries the busy A9; the other, which you cross, is a footbridge beside it. From the road and also from the bridge you will often see fishermen in small boats out on the loch. Once across the footbridge, turn right and retrace your outward route back to the dam. The power station and its famous fish ladder, built (like the one on the Tummel) to allow salmon to pass upriver to spawn, are open to visitors and are well worth a visit either now or later during your stay in the area.

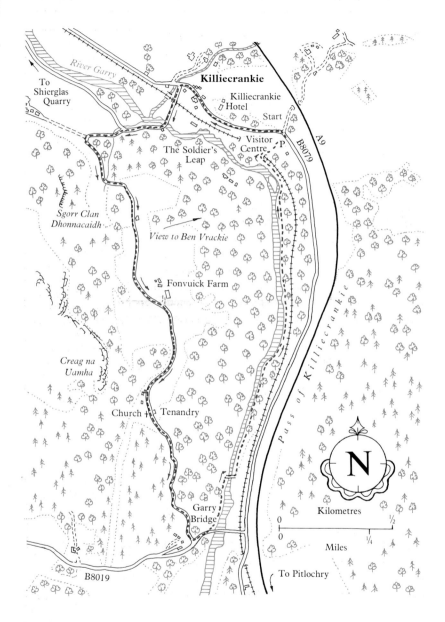

River Garry

To
Shierglas
Quarry

Killiecrankie

Killiecrankie
Hotel

Start

Visitor
Centre P

The Soldier's
Leap

B8079

A9

Sgorr Clan
Dhonnacaidh

View to Ben Vrackie

Fonvuick Farm

Creag na
Uamha

Church

Tenandry

Pass of Killiecrankie

N

Garry
Bridge

Kilometres

0   ½

0   ¼

Miles

B8019

To Pitlochry

KILLIECRANKIE AND TENANDRY

This straightforward circuit is largely on quiet roads, but is no less enjoyable for that. It takes in the Pass of Killiecrankie, noted for the 1689 battle and today for its abundant wildlife and fine trees, and a lovely old church. The walk starts from the National Trust for Scotland Visitor Centre at Killiecrankie, 5km north of Pitlochry. You can visit the excellent Centre first if you wish, but I suggest doing the walk first, as this will give you a fuller appreciation of the story told in the Centre.

From the Visitor Centre, turn left (north) along the road. Keep close to the left-hand verge, as this first short section of road can be quite busy, especially in high summer. Pass the entrance to the Killiecrankie Hotel and continue down the road, noting the steep drop to the gorge on your left. The road enters Killiecrankie village, which happily retains its post office and shop and has regular bus links with Pitlochry.

Turn left (at the RSPB sign) and cross the railway and the River Garry. There is an interesting contrast between the upstream side, where the river is open and broad, and downstream where it enters the gorge and flows swiftly between huge boulders. When the road forks keep left (the right fork leads to the large Shierglas Quarry near Blair Atholl) and at the next junction, turn left on to the Tenandry road.

The steep crag on the right, with trees somehow clinging tenaciously to it, is Sgorr Clan Dhonnacaidh. Families within this clan, which has its own museum at Calvine on the A9 north of Blair Atholl, include Reid, Robertson, MacConnachie, Duncan and MacInroy. The lane winds round, fringed with birch trees and with fine views of Ben Vrackie away to the left.

As it climbs, you have the opportunity to pause and look back to the north-east to the hills of the Beinn y Ghlo group, which includes three Munros (peaks over 914 m/3000 ft). The principal summit rejoices in the name of Braigh Coire Chruinn-bhalgain, which translates as 'upland of the corrie of round blisters', a

INFORMATION

Distance: 8 km (5 miles).

Start and finish: NTS Visitor Centre, Killiecrankie.

Terrain: Roads and good tracks. No special footwear needed.

Refreshments: At the Visitor Centre (Apr–Oct).

Opening hours NTS Visitor Centre, Killiecrankie: 1 Apr–31 Oct daily, 0930–1800 Jun–Aug, otherwise 1000–1700. Admission charge for non-members. Rangers regularly lead walks – details at the Centre or from the tourist information centre in Pitlochry.

The River Garry.

typically evocative Gaelic topographical name. The hill facing you is more simply named, as Carn Liath – 'grey hill' – which is certainly apt.

Just past Fonvuick Farm, a marshy area on the left just by the road is enriched with lovely orchids in summer. The crag now up to the right is Creag na Uamha, which means 'crag of caves'. It is a common name in Scotland. Away to the left you can see the traffic speeding along the A9. Be grateful you're up here! As you reach Tenandry, there is a superb copper beech tree beside the road, then you see the kirk, which is normally open to visitors. Its interior is fairly plain, but it has a long and interesting history. The name Tenandry comes from the Gaelic *an t-seanaontachd*, meaning 'the old agreement'.

Left: The imposing railway viaduct.

Right: Tenandry Church.

The church dates from 1836. It was built after Mrs Christian Hay of Seggieden, owner of the Tenandry estate, and her sister Miss Stewart approached the Society for the Propagation of Christian Knowledge, offering land for a church. The proposal was agreed by the General Assembly of the Church of Scotland in 1835 and the church was built with seating for 400 worshippers, the minister's stipend being set at £85 per annum.

William Grant from Nairn was chosen as the first minister, and served until 1843, preaching in both English and Gaelic. He left at the time of the Disruption, when the church establishment in Scotland was riven by disagreement over patronage – the rights of heritors (such as Mrs Hay and Miss Stewart) to nominate and approve ministers.

Peace was restored in 1850 when Pat Grant arrived, to start a ministry that was to last for 38 years. Tenandry continued to be ministered separately until 1954, when the parish was linked with Foss and Tummel. This link was severed in 1978, and since 1981 Tenandry has been what is called a 'continuing vacancy', with a number of ministers presiding over the weekly services. On 15 June 1986, the then Moderator of the General Assembly, Dr Robert Craig, preached at Tenandry to mark the kirk's 150th anniversary.

This is a lovely peaceful spot at which to pause, perhaps on the seat dedicated to the memory of Helen Victoria Barbour of Fincastle, who died in 1982 aged 91. The kirkyard contains some interesting and curious stones, including one remembering Norman Walker, Sheriff, who was born in Cumberland in 1889 and died at St Andrews in 1975. Maybe he took his holidays here and grew to love the place?

From the kirk continue downhill along the lane, now in the woods again. Meet the B8109 and turn left. At the high bridge over the Garry, go down steps to the left. The bridge is very impressive from below. Continue on a surfaced path (this was the road before the new bridge was built) and turn right over a footbridge with fine views up the gorge. Turn left, and left again in 80m on the riverside path, noting the old milestone with its legend 'Blair Atholl 3, Tummel Bridge 11'.

Continue along by the river, enjoying the rush of the water and the fine trees. There is plentiful birdlife along here including finches, dippers, crows and perhaps a buzzard with its distinctive mew. You pass below the splendid railway viaduct designed by the noted engineer John Mitchell, completed in 1863 at a cost of £5730. You could add a couple of noughts to that figure today. The viaduct is 155m (510ft) long and reaches a height of 16.5m (54ft).

The path begins to climb. At a junction go left to the Soldier's Leap, then on and up to the right to the path leading across to the Visitor Centre. Wild honeysuckle is often found in this area.

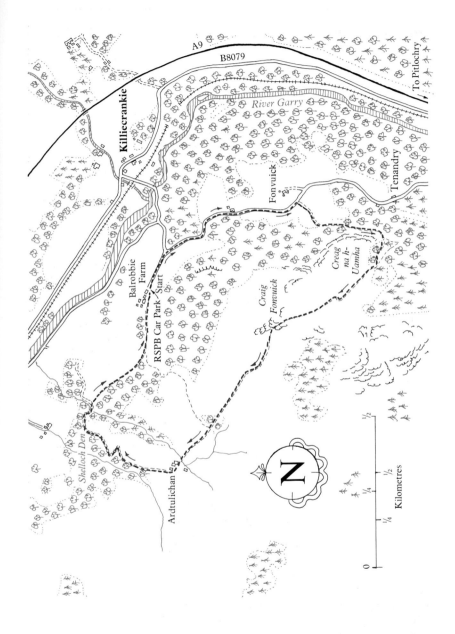

KILLIECRANKIE RESERVE

The Royal Society for the Protection of Birds' reserve at Killiecrankie, rising from the west bank of the River Garry, covers 530 hectares of mixed woodland, crag and open hill. There is a permanent warden at Balrobbie Farm, and from the small car park here, two overlapping walks are laid out. A board in the car park gives seasonal information on some of the birds you may see on the walk, and a guide to the reserve can be obtained. Around the walk there are boards giving further information on animals, birds and plants.

From the car park, which commands a very fine view of Ben Vrackie, walk back down the access track and at the road junction, turn right. From here to Fonvuick the route is the same as on the Tenandry circuit (walk 3), but instead of merely admiring the crags to the right, you now have to face the prospect of climbing above them. The crags are home to jackdaws and stock doves, and ravens may also be seen.

INFORMATION

Distance: 7 km (4 miles).

Start and finish: RSPB car park, Balrobbie. Take the minor road through Killiecrankie, turn left in the village and follow RSPB signs to the car park.

Terrain: Road and path. Some sections can be muddy. Strong footwear advised.

Refreshments: None en route. Nearest in Killiecrankie.

Public transport: Local bus from Pitlochry to Killiecrankie village. Enquire at tourist information centre for times.

Opening hours The reserve is open dawn to dusk every day, free. Car parking charge of £1 for non-RSPB members.

Mist hangs over the reserve at Killiecrankie.

Just before Fonvuick, turn right (yellow arrow) through a gate and head left of the fence to pick up a path going round a grassy knoll. The path curves left to run below the crags. Turn right through the next gate then immediately left to walk along beside the dyke and fence. The path soon begins to climb as it winds round the slope, with views opening up towards Pitlochry. The path steepens, passes through an old iron gate and crosses a rushing burn. A bench here gives a welcome chance of a break, with a view across the bypass to Ben Vrackie.

Ben Vrackie dominates the skyline from many points on these walks.

The path turns sharp right and passes through an area rich in ferns. Among them are scaly male fern, beech fern and lemon scented fern – and of course the ubiquitous bracken, which in summer grows high on either side of the path. Among the summer birds to be seen and heard here are wood warblers and redstarts.

The path swings left below large crags and then takes a very sharp turn right to continue up through birchwood and then larch. Birds hereabouts may include coal tits, chaffinches, redstarts and crossbills and roe deer are often seen in the sheltered hollow ahead. The hollow is in fact the former croft of Corhulichan, and the path crosses it on its right side to reach the ruins of the buildings. This is a good place for a stop, to pause and reflect on the way of life of the people who tended livestock, grew crops and made a living a hundred years and more ago. It is a quiet and peaceful place now.

Not long after passing the ruins, the path reaches its highest point at a lone pine. There are superb views in both directions: back to Loch Faskally and Deuchary Hill and, after a few more paces, forward to Glen Garry with Blair Castle in the centre of the picture. After this the path starts to descend. The vegetation has changed to heather moor, and you may see grouse in this area. Before long Beinn y Ghlo is seen to the right.

The path goes through a birch wood, which displays superb colouring in spring, when it is a vivid fresh green, and in autumn, when it glows golden against the sky. Cross a fence by a stile and continue to the edge of the wood. You can turn right here (yellow/green markers) for a short cut back to the car park, but the full walk continues across the field, now following green markers.

Go through a gate and pass to the right of the buildings at Ardtulichan, occupied by RSPB staff, though livestock are still kept in the fields. A feature of the reserve is that farming and conservation work together, with the grazing managed so that the farmer and the wildlife both benefit.

Frosted trees lend a winter glitter to the scene.

Cross a stile and go half right to join a grass track. To the left is Shelloch Den, its steep sides birch-clad. You can often see red squirrels here. Follow the track as it twists downhill, making a big swing to the right and crossing a burn. In a further 50 m, go right and cross a stile to walk beside a dyke. Cross another stile and turn right for 75 m, then left across the burn and up beside another dyke. On the hill here are several exclosures, areas fenced off to allow natural regeneration to take place. You can see the difference when grazing pressure is lifted.

Go through a gate, rejoining the yellow route, and walk along beside a fence and dyke. All this area is rich in flowers including orchids in summer. The path passes behind the buildings at Balrobbie to return to the car park, where as well as the reserve guide, general information on RSPB is available. If you are not already a member, perhaps you might be tempted to join to support the very worthwhile work the Society carries out all over the country on reserves such as this.

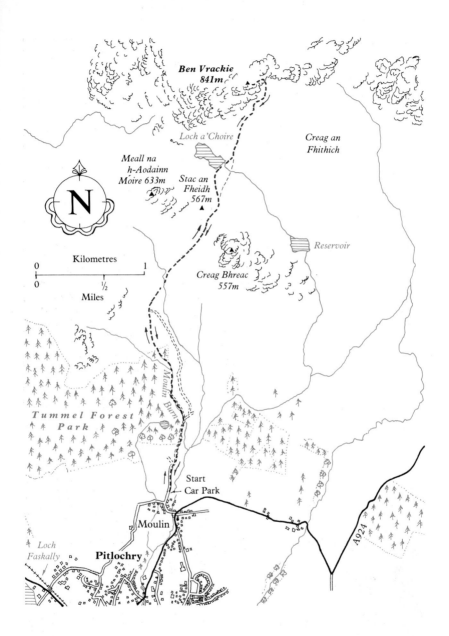

BEN VRACKIE

Walk out of the upper end of the car park, and follow the path, soon joining an estate track for about 200 m before leaving it again to resume on the path which rises steadily beside the Moulin Burn through mixed woodland. At the edge of the wood, cross the stile on to open moorland and gaze with anticipation at the scene ahead. The summit is hidden at this point but you can see the path curving away uphill and over the immediate horizon.

Follow the path, which soon provides extensive views back down the Tummel/Tay Valley. Before long you reach a memorial plaque to an Australian airman, and this is a good place to pause and take in the surroundings. The small craggy hill up on the right is Creag Bhreac. Interestingly, this name, meaning 'speckled crag', is the same as Ben Vrackie ('speckled hill'), despite the different spelling. In the latter case, Bhreac (pronounced Vreck) has become corrupted into Vrackie over a long period of time. There are many hills of this name in Scotland.

INFORMATION

Distance: 12 km (7 miles).

Start and finish: The small car park sign-posted from the village of Moulin, 3 km north-east of Pitlochry on the A924 Braemar road.

Terrain: Paths. Steep climb towards the summit. The walk should only be undertaken in good conditions unless you are an experienced hillwalker. Boots must be worn and good waterproofs, food and spare warm clothing carried.

Refreshments: None en route. Wide choice in Pitlochry, also the Moulin Inn.

Ben Vrackie from Loch a'Choire.

The path continues climbing, with a fence on the right, rounding a corner below the small bluff called Stac an Fheidh ('peak of deer') to see Loch a'Choire ahead. The main path passes over a stretch of frequently very boggy ground to the right of the loch but it is easy to make a diversion to walk over its impounding dam.

From here you can see the upper part of the hill rising more steeply ahead. The spur over to the right is Creag an Fhithich, 'crag of ravens'.

Take a deep breath and start the hard part of the ascent. If, as I hope, you have chosen a fine day, there is no need to hurry. It's not a race and you will get there in the end. Views are opening out all the time, with glimpses of the bigger hills to the north and the fine panorama back to the south always ready to catch your eye.

The Beinn y Ghlo group from the summit of Ben Vrackie.

The path winds up, pressing relentlessly on and heading for the right of the summit. It goes up into a high corrie and then turns back left for the final push up to the 841m summit, with its triangulation pillar, cairn and view indicator. And what a view it is! In clear weather it seems that half of Scotland is spread out below you.

To the north-west, across Glen Girnaig, are the triple peaks of Beinn y Ghlo, with Carn Liath, the nearest, showing by its extensive screes why it is called 'grey hill'. Further round, you look up the glen of the River Garry towards the Drumochter Pass, along the line taken by General Wade when he made his military road to Fort George at Inverness in the 1730s, the same line followed by both the A9 and the railway today.

Over to the west is the Tay Forest Park and further away the unmistakable cone of Schiehallion. The panorama is completed by the broad strath of Tummel and Tay leading south towards Dunkeld. It is a place to linger (provided the wind is not too cold) and savour, though you are unlikely to have it to yourself, for Vrackie is a deservedly popular hill.

On one of her first visits to Scotland, Queen Victoria stayed at Blair Castle in 1844 and enjoyed a number of tours about the countryside here, climbing several hills. She mentions Ben Vrackie, and was clearly much impressed by the beauty of the Highland scene. These expeditions greatly influenced her decision, taken with Prince Albert, to buy the Balmoral Estate on Deeside.

The return is by the same path, and again it pays to take your time and enjoy the experience to the full. At 841 m (2760 ft), Ben Vrackie is not quite a Munro, the name given to Scottish hills over 914 m/3000 ft, but it is a fine hill for all that and has a panorama not matched by many hills of greater height.

Somewhere on your expedition you may come across the Vrackie goats. A small group of adult goats have claimed the hill as their own. Nominally wild, they have learned that people carry food and are prone to nudging you for a titbit. They are harmless and rather fun to meet – and photograph! – but giving them food is not encouraged. If you do so they will only follow you wanting more, and they are not short of natural food on the hill.

This is not a hillwalking guide, but if your ascent of Ben Vrackie has whetted your appetite there are many excellent books and guides available describing the superlative mountains of Scotland. Or you may be perfectly content with just this one. Either way, you will have enjoyed a fine day out on a grand hill.

Wild goats are often seen on the hill.

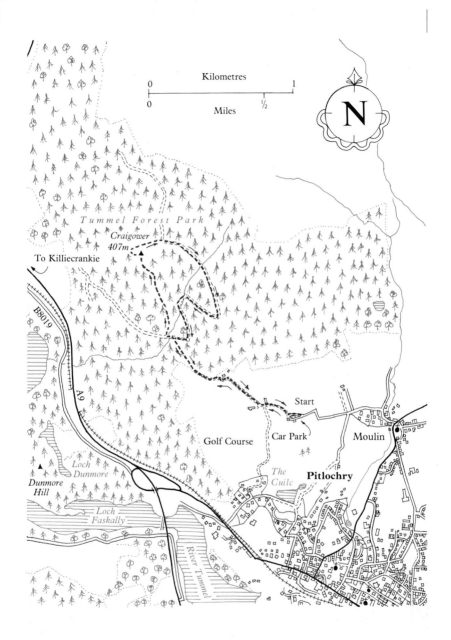

Kilometres
0   1

Miles
0   ½

N

Tummel Forest Park

Craigower
407m

To Killiecrankie

B8019

A9

Loch
Dunmore

Dunmore
Hill

Loch
Faskally

River Tummel

Golf Course

Car Park

Start

The
Cuilc

Moulin

Pitlochry

CRAIGOWER

The walk follows the Dunmore Trail path and leads up to a notable viewpoint. The upper part of Craigower, extending for 4.5ha, was given to the National Trust for Scotland in 1947 by the late Mrs Fergusson of Baledmund in memory of her father, Captain Wisely. The Dunmore Trail is named in memory of John, Earl of Dunmore, a member of the Trust's council and its executive committee, who died in 1980, and of his father, Viscount Fincastle, who was killed in action in 1940.

From the car park follow the road towards the golf course, which must surely be one of the most scenic courses anywhere in Britain. Golfers must have to concentrate hard to play their shots without being distracted by the views. Fortunately you only have to walk, look and enjoy.

Cross a fairway as signposted, exercising care and crossing only when there are no golfers playing on the hole, pass the fourth tee and turn left in front of Rock Cottage. Mrs Shirley-Anne Hardy, who lives here, is noted for her radical views on land use and ownership, and has published booklets and articles on the subject.

INFORMATION

Distance: 7 km (4 miles).

Start and finish: The small Craigower car park, reached by taking the A924 Braemar road out of Pitlochry to Moulin. Turn left behind the Moulin Hotel and follow the Craigower signs until a grass car park is reached next to a cottage.

Terrain: Good tracks and paths. No special footwear needed.

Refreshments: None en route. Wide choice in Pitlochry.

Craigower with the Atholl hills beyond.

There is already a fine view back down the valley of the Tay, over Pitlochry towards Ballinluig. Enter the wood at a kissing gate and walk along with a stone dyke on your left, still beside the golf course. The path then turns right into the wood proper, much of which is conifer planting. Meet a forest road, turn left for a few metres then right by a picnic table along a good path climbing through tall conifers.

The path emerges from the wood with the summit of the hill rearing up ahead. Go right and steeply up a smaller path, curving round to reach the summit. A viewpoint indicator shows what can be seen and explains the different types of land use in the area – agriculture, forestry and grouse moor. Conservation could perhaps be added to that list as you are standing on a hill owned by Scotland's premier conservation body.

It is not hard to see why Craigower was a 'beacon hill' in the times when messages were passed in this way, from hilltop to hilltop. The panorama is truly outstanding. To the west, a superb long view encompasses Loch Tummel and the distant peaks around Rannoch Moor, with Glencoe visible in clear conditions. To the left is the cone of Schiehallion. Turning right, the view extends up the Pass of Killiecrankie to Blair Atholl and beyond, with the massif of Beinn y Ghlo at far right. The valley with its traffic seems far below.

Start the return as waymarked, down a path to the right. Ben Vrackie can soon be seen ahead. The path winds through a rather dense plantation to reach the forest road. Turn right past a large Cellnet aerial and follow the road as it twists steadily downhill round several bends. Just when you are wondering which way you are facing, the outward route is rejoined near the picnic table. Turn left and walk down past the golf course, across the fairway and back to the car park.

Opposite: Faskally House and Craigower Hill.

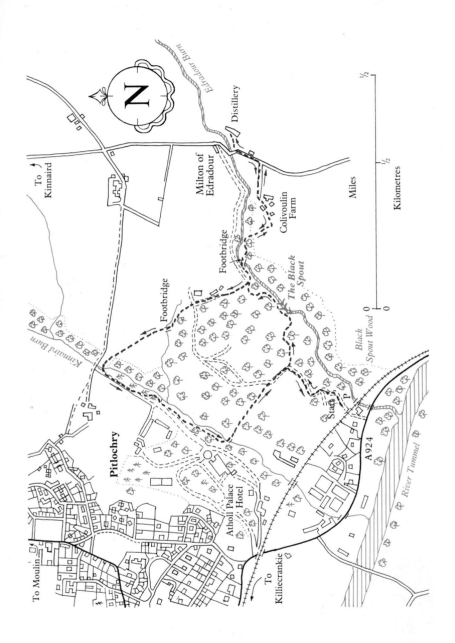

THE BLACK SPOUT
AND EDRADOUR

This varied walk takes in a fine waterfall and an intriguing distillery which is open to visitors. From the car park, turn right following the Black Spout sign, and at the fork keep right. The imposing turrets of the Atholl Palace Hotel appear over the trees to the left.

At the next junction turn right following a signpost to the Black Spout and Edradour, and climb steadily through a beautiful mature wood of oak and birch. At another fork, go right to reach the viewing platform for the Black Spout. The platform has been provided by the Rotary Club of Pitlochry and was built by Aberdeen University OTC in July 1989.

INFORMATION

Distance: 6 km
(3 ½ miles).

Start and finish:
Black Spout Wood car park, signposted off the main road at the south end of Pitlochry.

Terrain: Paths and tracks. Strong footwear needed in wet conditions.

Refreshments: Wide selection in Pitlochry, plus your free dram at Edradour!

Opening hours:
Edradour Distillery: Mar–Oct, Mon–Sat 0930–1700. Shop only, Nov–Feb, Mon–Sat 1030–1600.

The Black Spout falls.

It provides a spectacular view of the triple fall, which is seen at its best after a period of rain. A short top fall drops to a dark pool, then the longer central fall thunders down to another pool. Finally a waterslide over rocks brings the cataract to the burn at the foot of the gorge. The total drop is around 60m and it makes a splendid sight and sound.

Left: Spray from the falls makes a dramatic picture.

Right: The distillery at Edradour.

From the falls, go uphill through the woods (signposted Edradour), passing the lip of the falls. The path winds around as if unsure which direction to take. When the path forks go right, and at the field corner go down half-right to a neat little footbridge over the burn which feeds the falls. Carry on to a small gate, go through it and up the bank (the path is indistinct here) with a fence on your right and very good views down Strath Tummel. Go through two gates and turn left (look for the yellow arrow) to walk up past Colivoulin Farm to the road. The farm name means 'mill wood', indicating that the rushing burn once powered a mill here, and indeed the settlement is still named Milton of Edradour on today's maps.

At the road, turn left for a few metres to the distinctive buildings of Edradour Distillery. Founded in 1825, it prides itself on being the smallest distillery in Scotland and the last to produce a handcrafted malt whisky in limited quantity. The essential ingredients for whisky are water and grain. Edradour's water comes from high on Moulin Moor, based on granite, and passes through peat to give it a special character. The distillery uses local barley, malted and dried over peat fires.

There are regular tours so that visitors can see the distilling process, starting with the mash tun, where water and barley are soaked together to make 'wort', which then ferments with brewer's yeast. The mixture, now called 'wash', goes to the stills. The copper stills at Edradour are the smallest size permitted under Excise rules. The stillman's skill in selecting the spirit is a vital part of the whole process.

The end product is 150 gallons (650 litres) a week of a clear spirit, 70 degree proof. It is matured in sherry casks specially imported from Spain for at least ten years before being bottled. At the end of your tour you can taste the result and appreciate why the Gaelic name for whisky is *uisgebaugh*, 'the water of life'. Edradour has an excellent shop where souvenirs can be bought.

Fortified by your dram, continue the walk by returning past Colivoulin into the wood, over the footbridge and up to the field corner. There is a fine view from here taking in Ben Vrackie and Craigower and down across the golf course.

Do not go back down through the wood but instead go right (signposted Moulin), passing cottages to another junction. Go ahead again, still following signs to Moulin. A seat here gives another good view of Ben Vrackie. Cross a small burn by a footbridge and then take a field path on the right. This type of path, common in England and Wales, is quite unusual in Scotland.

Re-enter the wood and cross another burn, then turn left (signposted Pitlochry) and walk down beside the Kinnaird Burn, passing beneath some magnificent old larch trees, then seeing a small waterfall on your left. Fork left, across the burn, then left and right (signposted to Black Spout) to rejoin the track leading down to the car park.

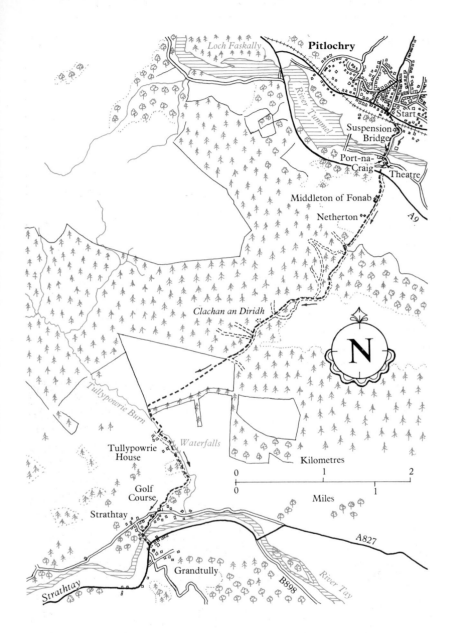

PITLOCHRY TO STRATHTAY

This lovely walk is deservedly popular with both locals and visitors. From the War Memorial in Pitlochry town centre, walk across the small park towards its left-hand corner and go under the railway bridge. Swing left with the road and take the path that climbs right, over the wee burn, then follow the Festival Theatre sign to the left.

Cross the road by the showground and take the path signposted to the Festival Theatre over a fine suspension bridge crossing the River Tummel. A notice warns against cycling, loitering or swinging on the bridge, but a pause to take in the view is permissible, I think!

Upstream is the dam impounding Loch Faskally, and across the river is the settlement of Port-na-Craig. You will see that the first house is called Ferryman's Cottage (now a guest house and snack bar). There were many ferries across Scotland's rivers in the times before bridges were frequent, and the names of many such places have survived.

INFORMATION

Distance: 8 km (5 miles).

Start: Pitlochry.

Finish: Grandtully Hotel. Bus back to Pitlochry (enquire at tourist information centre for times).

Terrain: Mostly good tracks and paths. A small amount of open country. Special footwear only needed in wet conditions.

Refreshments: Grandtully Hotel, or Pitlochry.

Looking over Pitlochry to Ben Vrackie.

Down by the far bank is a brick pillar with a water level gauge and instruments atop it. This is a gauging station operated by the Tay River Purification Board for measuring water flow. It records the flow every half hour and is linked to a central computer in the Board's headquarters in Perth. These gauging stations become vitally important during times of flood, such as happened in January 1993 following a week of heavy snowfall, rapid thaw and torrential rain.

At 5.15 a.m. on Saturday 16 January, a flow of 1047 cubic metres per second (cumecs) was recorded here, the highest ever at this station (an average daily maximum would be between 150 and 200 cumecs), and at that time the water was 5.1 m above gauge zero. Add that to all the water rushing down the Tay and it is little wonder that much of the farmland in this area was inundated and Perth itself was severely affected.

These things rarely affect the visitor but they are a reminder of the awesome power of nature. Continue over the bridge and on reaching the road turn left, or go straight over if you wish to visit the Festival Theatre, which presents six different plays every summer season. If you do visit the theatre, which has a coffee shop, bar and restaurant, return through the car park.

The stones at Clachan an Diridh.

Cross the junction and follow the lane uphill (signposted 'public footpath to Strathtay'). Now comes the most dangerous part of the walk – crossing the very busy A9. Take your time and cross WITH GREAT CARE, continuing up the lane opposite to pass through Middleton of Fonab farm and on uphill along a track between fences. Past Netherton, pause at the gate for a splendid view back over Pitlochry. Ben Vrackie is unfortunately blocked by a large tree.

The track continues climbing steadily to enter woodland and zigzags up through the trees. *Now* there is a fine view back to Ben Vrackie! Turn left on the path as signposted, go through a gate and continue, still climbing, with pines to the right and a birchwood to the left. The lovely old grassy path winds up, and you soon see a heather moor to the left, glorious in rich purple in autumn.

Note: When timber operations are being carried out, this path may be closed. If so please follow diversion signs.

Meet and cross a broad track at a waymarker and take the grass path leading up beside it to its right. This parallels the track for a while then swings right, away from it, over a rise. At the junction of tracks go straight ahead. In a further 150 m, take a small path on the right to see Clachan an Diridh, a small group of much weathered standing stones. The name may mean 'the upright stones' but little is known of their history. I always feel a tremendous sense of atmosphere at such places, knowing the stones have stood here for thousands of years.

Return to the track and continue. A stone dyke comes in from the left before the forest road swings left. Do not follow it, but go straight ahead over a ladder stile with a grand view up Strathtay. The path continues over open pasture with Farragon Hill prominent to the right. The path is quite clear at this stage.

After about 400 m, go through a gateway and continue with a fence on your right, going gently downhill. There is a multiplicity of paths here made by people, vehicles and livestock: keep high, by the fence until its corner, then go past the end of a birchwood (marker pole) then ahead, passing two more waymarkers, through an area of gorse to turn left through a gate and walk down beside the Tullypowrie Burn.

There are lots of lovely small waterfalls and several grassy areas ideal for a stop. Continue down through a gully and then beside a fence and the wall of Tullypowrie House to walk first beside a stone dyke and then between dykes along a shady path with overhanging trees.

The path eventually emerges to cross the 8th fairway of Strathtay Golf Club – take due care! Continue down, through a gate on to a short lane which leads to the road in Strathtay village. If you turn right here and then take the left fork, you will reach the River Tay in about 400 m at a point where there is a canoe slalom course. It is great fun to watch the canoeists, and sometimes rafts, coming down through the white water.

Shooting the rapids at
Grandtully.

Across the bridge is Grandtully with its hotel (drinks and meals), public toilets and the bus back to Pitlochry.

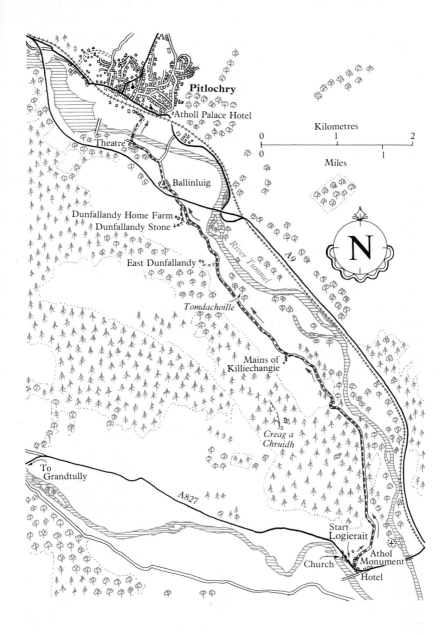

ROB ROY AND THE PICTS

Although this walk is all on roads it has plenty of interest and there is generally little traffic to trouble the walker. Start by visiting Logierait's neat church. There has been a church or chapel on this site since the 7th century. The present building dates from 1805 and was renovated in 1928 and again in 1971, internally, and also reharled in 1991. A stone on the church wall behind the porch commemorates Alexander Mackenzie, born here in 1822, who became the first Prime Minister of Canada. Another, more recent son of the parish who has achieved fame is Dennis Mann, whose engraved glass trophies are given to the winner of the popular BBC television quiz *Mastermind* each year.

There is a Pictish cross in the kirkyard dating back to the 10th century and also three 'mortsafes', cages used to protect graves from bodysnatchers in the early 19th century when unscrupulous people sold corpses to medical schools. There are also a number of memorial stones to members of the Butter family, notable locally for many generations. Sir David Butter is the present Lord Lieutenant of Perthshire.

The name Logierait seems to be accepted by linguistic scholars as a corruption of *Lagan m-Choid*, 'the hollow of St Coed', who founded the first church here. Logierait is notable today for having a lady minister, the Rev. Irene Miller.

INFORMATION

Distance: 7 km (4 miles).

Start: Logierait village, reached by bus from Pitlochry – enquire at the tourist information centre for times.

Finish: Pitlochry.

Terrain: All on roads. No special footwear needed.

Refreshments: Logierait Inn, wide choice in Pitlochry.

Logierait Church.

Leave the church and walk back through the village, noting, behind the Logierait Hotel, the bridge across the Tay which carried the former railway line from Aberfeldy. The branch from Ballinluig was opened in July 1865, with stations at Balnaguard and Grandtully, and lasted exactly 100 years before falling victim to the Beeching cuts in May 1965. Some parts of the old line are walkable but much has sadly been lost.

The impressive Atholl monument.

Turn left up the minor road signposted to Dunfallandy, Clunie and Foss. It climbs steeply for a short while before levelling out past a neat small cemetery, and then becomes a narrow lane with little traffic. To the right, peeping out of the trees, you can see a stone cross. This is the top of a large and impressive monument to the 6th Duke of Atholl, erected on this site in 1866 'by the inhabitants of Athole and numerous friends in testimony of their regard and esteem for his character'. A rather overgrown path leads up to the monument from the riverbank but it is not accessible from this side.

Also in this area was Logierait's old castle, which has associations with Rob Roy MacGregor, who you will find, if you read his true story, was not at all the fearsome brigand and outlaw he has been made out to be. He was a man of his time, and that was a time of much rivalry between factions in Scotland. Rob had enemies, as did many others like him.

In 1717 Rob had fallen out with the then Duke of Atholl, who managed to capture him at Dunkeld through a subterfuge and brought him to Logierait under heavy escort on 3 June of that year. Within three days Rob was free. One of his clansmen brought a message, supposedly from Rob's wife, and the guards, whom Rob had taken care to flatter and amuse, were less vigilant than they should have been. They let Rob out of the door to read the message and in a flash he was on his clansman's horse and away. The Duke, who had already boasted of capturing Rob, was naturally mortified. 'Roy' in his name comes from the Gaelic *ruadh* meaning red – as it does in the placenames Glen Roy and Roy Bridge near Fort William.

Continue along the road, with a beautiful view of Ben Vrackie framed in trees. There is forestry to the left and high above pylons you can see Creag a'Chruidh (possibly 'crag of the Picts', from the Gaelic *Cruithnigh* for that race). The road winds round several bends before reaching Woodend Cottage, after which it dips and then climbs quite steeply past Mains of Killiechangie, which has a quite splendid prospect over Strath Tummel to Pitlochry, with the Atholl Palace Hotel prominent, and Ben Vrackie rising behind the town. The placename seems to be derived from 'the cell of Coemhi', an obscure Celtic saint.

Left and below:
The Dunfallandy Stone,
passed on this walk.

After this the road passes through attractive birchwood. The trend is now definitely downhill but there is one more short climb before Tomdachoille ('wooded hill') is passed. There are plenty of blackberries along here – good for an autumn walk!

Past East Dunfallandy with its collection of caravans the road emerges into the open again with the A9 bridge over the Tummel to the right and again a fine view over Pitlochry to the hills. At the entry to Dunfallandy Home Farm, go left and follow the signs to view the Dunfallandy Stone in its protective glass case. The stone is thought to date from the 9th century. The front is a cross of ornamental panels flanked by angels and beasts. On the back, framed by two serpents, are seated figures and enigmatic Pictish symbols. Much research has been done on these stones in recent years but in truth they remain as mysterious as the people who carved them.

Return to the road and turn left to pass under the A9. Go through the hamlet of Ballinluig, noting that the name is the same as that of the village a few kilometres south. This is not uncommon in Scotland. At the junction, turn left, and at the next junction, with the Festival Theatre ahead, go right and right again over the suspension bridge, into the centre of Pitlochry.

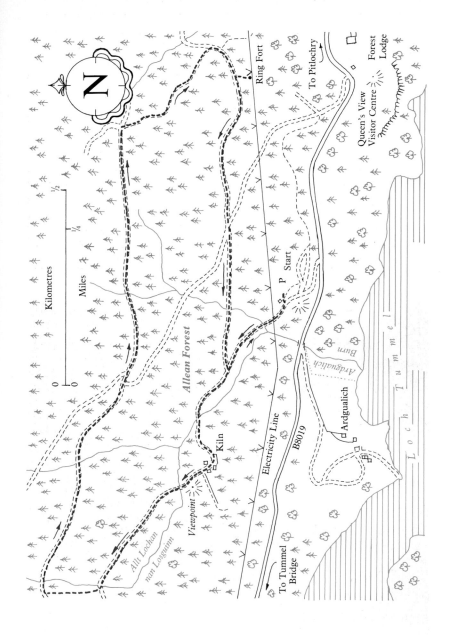

ALLEAN FOREST

This short but nonetheless interesting walk is one of a number laid out in the Tay Forest Park by Forest Enterprise. From the car park, follow the main forest track uphill. The walk, known as the Ring Fort Walk, follows red waymarkers all the way. The track climbs steadily, passing a junction with a red and white post and marker. This is not for a walk, but is part of a Wayfinding course. Wayfinding is the non-competitive introductory form of the navigational sport of orienteering: further details can be obtained at the Queen's View if you are interested.

The track continues climbing through mature conifers, passing another Wayfinding marker, to reach the old Clachan. This small settlement of three houses, small fields used for cultivation and a kiln for drying corn was probably established in the early 18th century and

INFORMATION

Distance: 5 km (3 miles).

Start and finish: Signposted car park 800 m west of the Queen's View Visitor Centre on B8019.

Terrain: Good forest tracks and paths. No special footwear needed.

Refreshments: None en route. Café at Queen's View.

The forest seen across Loch Tummel.

abandoned perhaps a hundred years later. It has a fine location on a south-facing slope and the inhabitants would have been largely self-sufficient, keeping a few sheep and cattle and growing their own crops and vegetables. After the breakdown of the clan system and the rise of large estates practising sheep-farming such places became impossible to sustain.

A path on the left leads in 200m to a viewpoint. Take away the forest and this would be the view enjoyed by the people of the Clachan, encompassing Loch Tummel and the hills around, topped by Schiehallion. The loch was lower until the 1950s, when its level was raised as part of a hydro-electric scheme. At the viewpoint is a wood sculpture by Charlie Easterfield showing a sleeping figure. It is one of a number in this area commissioned jointly by Forest Enterprise and Scottish Enterprise Tayside.

Top: Dramatic sculpture in the forest.

Above: Glorious autumn colours on the larches.

Return to the track, turn left and continue uphill. The trees soon become more mixed, with birch in among the pines. Birds to be seen and heard in the forest include siskin, crossbill, goldcrest and lesser redpoll: mammals include squirrels, foxes and both red and roe deer. The track swings right, crossing the Allt Lochan nan Losguinn twice (it is a small burn and not a major feature), and then opening out to give a wider view ahead. The track starts to descend gently, and after about 500m the yellow route goes off to the right.

Keep ahead, climbing a little. An open area on the right gives a fine view across the glen to Farragon Hill,

Beinn Eagagach and back to Schiehallion. Beinn
Eagagach is the scene of a controversial proposal to
open a mine for barytes, a mineral used in the offshore
oil industry. The plan went through a public inquiry in
summer 1993 and the outcome was still awaited at the
time this book went to press.

The old fort in the forest.

Reach a T-junction and turn right, leaving the track for
a pleasant grassy path that winds downhill to meet
another track. Turn right here. The loch is soon
glimpsed through the trees, and after 200 m, turn left as
signposted to view the ring fort. This ancient
stronghold, thought to date from the 8th century,
commands a tremendous view westward, unfortunately
rather spoiled by an overhead power line going right
through the site. The fort is about 10m in diameter
with thick walls, and the strengthened west gateway
can still clearly be seen.

Return to the track and turn left. It is all downhill now.
The yellow route comes down from the right at
Wayfinding marker no. 9, and the main track is then
soon visible ahead. Join it and walk back down to the
car park.

The Queen's View Visitor Centre is well worth a visit.
It has an excellent exhibition on forestry planning and
development, an audio-visual programme, a shop with
interesting souvenirs and books, a tearoom and toilets.
Also here is the Queen's View itself, admired by Queen
Victoria in 1866 but already named before that time, in
honour, it is thought, of Isabella, queen of Robert the
Bruce.

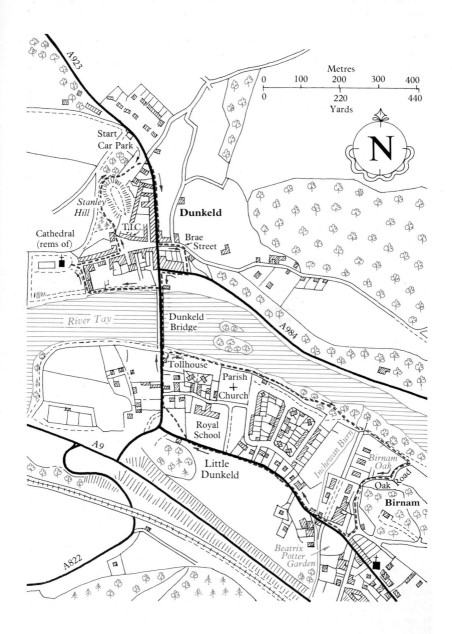

Metres
0   100   200   300   400
0   220   440
Yards

N

A923

Start
Car Park

Stanley
Hill

Cathedral
(rems of)

T.I.C.

Dunkeld

Brae
Street

River Tay

Dunkeld
Bridge

A984

Tollhouse

Parish
+ Church

Royal
School

Little
Dunkeld

A9

Inchewan Burn

Birnam
Oak

Oak Road

Birnam

A822

Beatrix
Potter
Garden

HISTORIC DUNKELD AND BIRNAM

There are many walks with literary associations, but there can be few which link, in a short step, two such startlingly different figures. Within a couple of minutes you pass from the medieval drama of Shakespeare's *Macbeth* to the enchanted world of Mrs Tiggywinkle, Jeremy Fisher and Peter Rabbit. Leave the car park to turn right towards the bridge over the Tay. The main street is full of interesting shops. Dunkeld was largely destroyed in a battle in 1689, but many of the buildings erected shortly after that time have been carefully preserved.

Turn left up Brae Street and climb steeply, but only for a short way, to the first gap on the right. Here is the Sundial House, named for the ancient sundial on its south-facing corner. Take the path right of the house and go carefully down steep and rather worn steps to the road. Cross *with great care* and turn right to reach the bridge. Opened in 1809, this is one of Thomas Telford's many magnificent engineering achievements in Scotland.

Walk over the bridge and at the far side, by the attractive old tollhouse, turn left down steps to the riverside. Turn right and walk along the riverside path (signposted to the Birnam Oak).

There are many fine trees along this stretch. Pass behind the parish church and cross the Inchewan Burn by a footbridge. Over the bridge go half-right then ahead on the main path to reach the Birnam

INFORMATION

Distance: About 5 km (3 miles).

Terrain: Pavements and good paths. No special footwear needed.

Start and finish: Main car park, Dunkeld.

Toilets: In the main car park, in Birnam, and in the square beside the Tourist Information Centre.

Refreshments: Excellent selection of cafés and hotels in both Dunkeld and Birnam.

Opening Hours
Dunkeld Cathedral: Apr–Sept: Mon–Sat 0930–1900, Sun 1400–1900. Oct–Mar: Mon–Sat 0930–1600, Sun 1400–1600.
Ell Shop: Jun–Aug: Mon–Sat 1000–1700, Sun 1400–1700. Apr–May and Sep–Dec: Mon–Sat 1000–1300, 1400–1700.
Scottish Horse Regimental Museum: Easter and Jun–Sept daily 1000–1200, 1400–1700.
Tourist Information Centre: Mar–Oct: daily 0930–1730. Nov–Feb: weekends only.

Telford's Bridge over the Tay in Dunkeld.

Oak, said to be the last survivor of the wood made famous by the witches' prophecy in *Macbeth*: 'fear not till Birnam Wood do come to Dunsinane'. The story is that in 1057 soldiers cut branches and foliage here to use as camouflage on their way to a battle at Dunsinane Hill, 20 km to the south-east.

Continue past the Oak for a short way to a flight of steps on the right. Climb the steps and pass to the right of Jubilee Park and play area. Turn right at its end and left into Oak Road to reach the centre of Birnam. The name, Norse in origin, means 'village of the warrior'. On the left here is a grocer's which sells its own delicious ice-cream, and on the right is the imposing Birnam Hotel. A typically grandiose Victorian building, it was opened in the 1850s, at the time that the railway reached Birnam. The row which includes the grocer's, Murthly Terrace, was built in the 1860s as summer lodges for visitors coming by train.

Peter Rabbit and family in the Beatrix Potter Garden.

Cross the road into the Beatrix Potter Garden, opened in 1992. There are imaginative sculptures of several of the famous characters from the children's stories. Beatrix spent many happy holidays in this area as a girl and young woman, and some of her best-loved characters are based on people she met at that time. After enjoying the garden, recross the road and turn left past imposing iron gates, crowned with four gilt lions. Walk past the driveway to the church and the Royal School of Dunkeld, founded in 1567. Go half right across a green and re-cross the bridge over the Tay.

Once over the bridge, turn sharply right and go down and under the bridge, then along the riverbank. From here you can see the full splendour of Telford's five-arched bridge, which after nearly 200 years looks as strong as ever. Continue on grass as far as the cathedral wall. Turn right and walk up to the gates to enter the cathedral grounds. The cathedral was begun in 1318; the nave and north-west tower date from the 15th century. Sacked during the Reformation, the church was reroofed in the 1660s, and still serves as the parish church for Dunkeld today. Its grounds contain many fine trees, including early examples of larches brought here in the 18th century.

The Cathedral gates in Dunkeld.

After visiting the cathedral, walk down Cathedral Street. You are now on the Dunkeld Heritage Trail. Many of the buildings have plaques giving interesting information. No. 9 was the childhood home of Alexander Mackenzie, later Prime Minister of Canada. On the corner of the main square is the Ell House, named for the ell measure – used in textiles – which is still affixed to its wall. Part of the building is now a shop, run by the National Trust for Scotland. The Trust, in association with local authorities, has restored many houses in Dunkeld to a very high standard. In the square is the Scottish Horse Regimental Museum, the ornate Atholl Memorial Fountain, the tourist information centre, and public toilets; on their left is the Duchess Anne, a building established in 1851 as a girls' school by Anne, Duchess of Atholl. It is now the church hall.

Pass through the gateway beside the toilets and walk around Stanley Hill, a tree-covered mound and open space given to the people of Dunkeld in 1958 by Cairngorm Investments. This may possibly be the dun or fort from which Dunkeld ('fort of the Caledonians') gets its name. At the far side of the hill you reach the car park and the end of the walk.

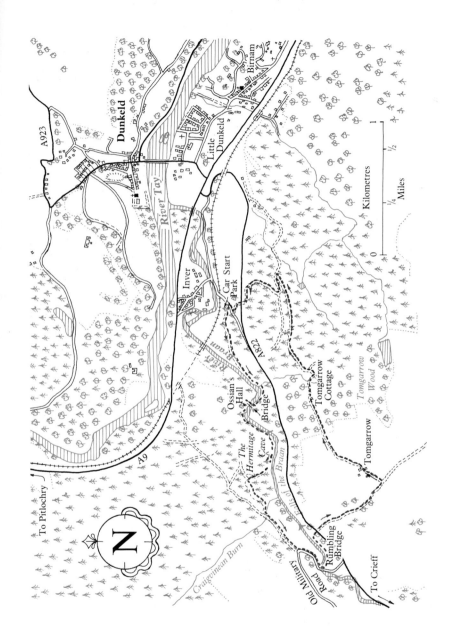

THE BRAAN AND RUMBLING BRIDGE

This very varied walk includes fine waterfalls, a historic track and excellent views. From the car park, take the signposted walk to The Hermitage. The walk goes through fine old woodland with some splendidly massive trees. The track is well used by mountain bikers, so be prepared to move aside to let them pass.

On reaching the lovely old 18th century bridge over the Braan, note the superb cedar of Lebanon towering over it, cross the bridge and then go up to look at the folly called Ossian's Hall. It was built in 1758 by the nephew of the 2nd Duke of Atholl (himself later the 3rd Duke) as a surprise for his uncle. The interior was decorated in 1783. At that time, visitors entered to see a painting of the bard Ossian singing to a number of lovely maidens. The waterfall could be heard but not seen until the guide operated a device which withdrew the painting into the wall, giving entry to a second room which was covered with mirrors, giving the extraordinary illusion of water pouring in every direction. The Hall was seriously damaged in 1869 but after being presented to the National Trust for Scotland, along with the surrounding woodland, in 1944 by Katharine, Duchess of Atholl, it was restored following a generous donation from Miss Marion Buchanan.

After viewing the folly – and the fine spectacle of the falls crashing down over the rocks below – continue westward along the riverside path, passing a seat dedicated to the memory of Frank McGowan, Archdeacon of Sarum (otherwise called Salisbury – a long way from here). A plantation of Norway spruce gives way to more open Scots pine. You may well see red squirrels in this area. Shredded pine cones on the ground show where they are active.

Continue past more falls to Ossian's Cave, a stone beehive hut with two entrances. Like the Hall, it has no real connection with Ossian but makes the basis of a nice story nonetheless. It was constructed around the time (1762) that James McPherson published his

INFORMATION

Distance: 8 km (5 miles).

Start and finish: Car park near Inver, reached by turning off the A9 on to the A822 Crieff road, then turning immediately right (signposted to Inver). After 400 m take the left fork, cross the railway, and the car park is 100 m ahead on the right.

Terrain: Paths, tracks and roads. Strong footwear recommended.

Refreshments: None en route. Nearest in Dunkeld or Birnam.

Opening hours: The Hermitage: Open all year, free.

The Hermitage and Falls of the Braan.

claimed translation of the poems of Ossian, the Celtic bard who sang of the great deeds of his warrior father Fingal. McPherson's works were later shown to be fakes, but there was a great enthusiasm for the Ossian story and many grottoes and follies were erected in his memory.

Carry on along the main path which after a further 200m begins to curve right, away from the river. The crowds have now been left behind and for the rest of the walk there will be fewer people about. Cross over a main track to join a path. After 150m curve left and in a further 50 m *turn* left onto a clear track. In about 200 m it briefly becomes a narrow path ducking through confining trees.

Autumn colours in the woods.

The track swings right then turns left to cross the Craigvinean Burn by a neat wooden footbridge (signposted to Rumbling Bridge). Continue on a wide grassy path across pasture. This is marked on maps as 'Old Military Road', a term commonly associated with General George Wade, who initiated the great road-building programme in the Highlands after the 1715 Rising. This path you are on is part of the route between Coupar Angus and Amulree, linking with the main routes up to Fort George (near Inverness) in the east and Fort William in the west.

As with many of these roads, it was Wade's successor, Major Caulfeild, who oversaw the building, in the 1740s. The path continues to meet a lane. The original line of the Military Road carried straight on towards Ballinloan (where the tenants blocked the road in 1751 while waiting for a new bridge), but this walk goes left, down to Rumbling Bridge, for the building of which the Commissioners of Roads granted the princely sum of £10 in 1774.

It was a job well done and the bridge is still sturdy today. On its right, the Braan crashes and thunders down big rock steps into its gorge, which is a long way below you to the left of the bridge.

Cross the bridge: there is access on the right to the rocks above the lip of the falls, and this is a *very* impressive place to stand.

Return to the road and after a further 50m take a small path into the woods on the left. It climbs and dips, then crosses two burns by footbridges, before swerving right to the A822 road. Cross with care and carry on along the track ahead (signposted as a public footpath to Glen Garr).

Follow the track as it climbs steadily. To the right (south) a fine view of distant Glendevon opens up. After about 400m a fence comes in from the left and continues as a stone dyke. Within a further 200 m, just before a cattle grid, turn left through a gate onto another track.

Past the settlement of Tomgarrow a splendid view northwards along the Tay Valley opens up. Continue with the track and enter Tomgarrow Wood, which mainly consists of old birches. Pass Tomgarrow Cottage, go right and left in quick succession, then continue for about 150 m before turning right over a small burn and through a gate in a high deer fence into conifer forest.

Dramatic lighting in Craigvinean Forest.

In 100 m turn left along a main track, and at a junction shortly after that continue straight over. Carry on along a broad track with a spruce plantation to the right and more fine northward views to the left. The gap made by the Tay through Dunkeld is very clear. In 700 m, at a major junction, go very sharply back left (a 180° turn). At the next junction in 200 m, continue right with the main track.

Keep with the track as it swings round left, downhill, then goes right through a gate to the A822. Cross *with great care* and follow the track ahead as it wriggles down to the minor road. The car park is a few paces to the right.

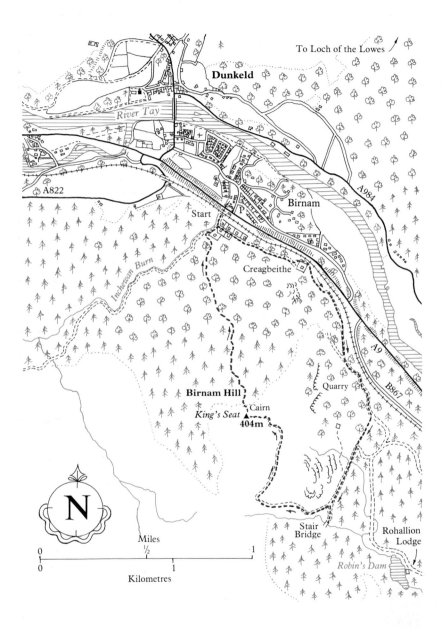

BIRNAM HILL

S tarting and finishing this walk at the railway station, as well as being logical, offers the opportunity for people based elsewhere to make this a convenient outing between trains. The walk goes to the top of a hill which is noted as a fine viewpoint, and also has associations with Macbeth.

From the railway station car park, head north and go down the steps to the path. Turn left and cross under the railway. The path emerges onto a road: go left, following the road sharply round to the left. Pass a number of fine detached houses including a splendid black-and-white painted house called Mullachmore, with the date 1899 at the top of the gable. There are plenty of rhododendrons around and the hillslope is often alive with rabbits.

Past the last house, Creagmor, on the left, the road becomes a track. At a turning circle there is a waymarker pointing ahead. The traffic on the A9 is very audible to your left at this point. Walk through very fine mature trees including a number of lovely old birches. The path is on a kind of shelf with the hill sloping down to your left and up – the way you are heading before long – to your right.

INFORMATION

Distance: 8 km (5 miles).

Start and finish: Dunkeld and Birnam railway station, just off the A9. If arriving by car, please park in Birnam village and walk up to the station.

Terrain: Minor road, tracks and paths. Some can be muddy in wet periods. Steep ascent and descent. Strong footwear essential.

Waymarked: Yes.

Refreshments: None en route. Wide selection in Dunkeld and Birnam.

Birnam Glen.

The path goes off to the left to pass behind the house called Creagbeithe ('birch crag'), and drops down markedly to a point quite close to the railway before starting to climb again, passing through open woodland. The path divides briefly, then the two paths rejoin before reaching a junction at an open grassy area. Go right over a small burn at the point where a seat offers a pleasant view across Dunkeld and the Tay.

The path soon begins to climb in earnest, and then drops down just as sharply towards the quarry car park. The quarry, up to the right, has very impressive sheer faces now somewhat masked by trees. Continue along a broad track and turn right uphill along a clear signposted path with dense undergrowth (especially in summer) to either side. The path continues climbing, going up to the right, to meet a track beside a stone dyke. Keep going uphill.

After about 250 m you pass a small grotto on the right with an attractive small burn running down through it and after a further 100 m a junction is reached with a sign saying King's Seat. Do not go up the branch path but continue with the track until the junction for Stair Bridge is reached. A diversion of only about 200 m here leads you down to the lovely old Stair Bridge, which commands a very fine view to Rohallion Lodge and the lake called Robin's Dam in front of the house. The burn which Stair Bridge crosses gurgles through a miniature gorge beneath you.

Return to the main track and turn left, still climbing steadily. In about 600 m it reaches a fence corner and swings right, with the summit of the hill now seen ahead and the views opening up. Curlew are often heard here between spring and autumn. Wind round with the track and then turn off to the left on a small path which threads its way up through rocks to the summit. A pause before the final ascent enables the still expanding view to be enjoyed again.

The last part of the climb is very steep, with steps to help you. The slope eases and the path winds first right and left before arriving at a large cairn where you can take in the full panorama over the Tay Valley in both

Fly Agaric can be seen in the woods.

directions and east to Loch of the Lowes and beyond. It is not quite possible to see Dunsinane Hill, to where Macbeth's forces are supposed to have marched, using branches taken from here as camouflage. One interesting point is that to retain the metre of the verse, Shakespeare has to have Dunsin*ane* pronounced with the stress on the last syllable, whereas locally it is said Duns*in*ane. Leaving aside the problems of writing heroic blank verse, the view is well worth the effort of attaining it, and at least you know that from here it is all downhill!

Leave the summit and start walking quite steeply down. The path winds around in a contorted manner but is always quite clear. It crosses a flatter, wet area before descending again. There are a number of reassuring waymarkers. An open area offers yet another fine view. As if fed up with all the twisting about, the path finally gathers itself for a headlong plunge downhill through fine mixed woodland with some splendid old trees including many birches.

Please take great care on this descent, as it is very easy to slip, especially if the ground is wet. There is no need to hurry. The path leads directly to the foot of the hill where you turn right beside the Inchewan Burn to return to the station.

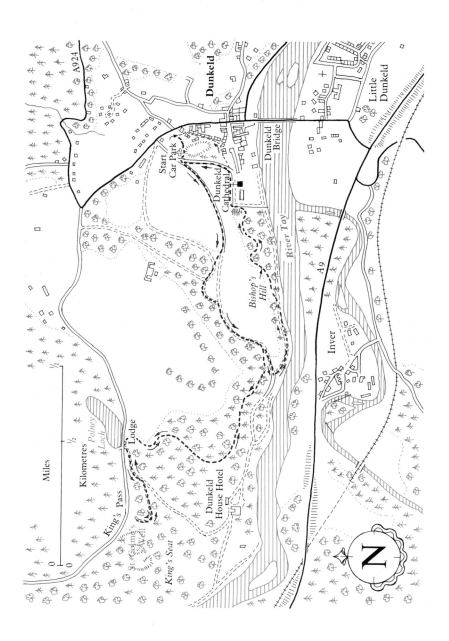

THE LARCH WALK

This walk is named for the fine trees first introduced to Scotland in this area over 200 years ago, but it has many other interesting features as well. It goes through part of the large estate now attached to Dunkeld House Hotel, currently owned by the Stakis Group and superbly placed beside the Tay.

From the car park, walk round the right-hand side of Stanley Hill and cross the grass half right to a gate giving access to the driveway of the hotel. Turn left and follow the drive (signposted Dunkeld Larches). It is better to walk on the grass verge rather than on the road.

The road runs alongside a large field which was the site of the original Dunkeld House, of which no trace now remains. It was here that in 1717, Rob Roy MacGregor was taken prisoner by the Duke of Atholl and then held briefly in Logierait Castle (see walk 9). Across the field you have a fine view of Dunkeld Cathedral.

INFORMATION

Distance: 6 km (4 miles).

Start and finish: Main car park in Dunkeld.

Terrain: Road, track and path. Some sections can be muddy in wet weather but special footwear is not usually needed.

Waymarked: Yes.

Refreshments: Wide choice in Dunkeld and at Dunkeld House Hotel. Toilets at the start.

Dunkeld Cathedral seen across the Tay.

On reaching a wood, go right, up into the trees along a small path which levels off to run along a terrace below magnificent old beech trees for about 200m before joining another road. Turn left with the road and curve back down to join the hotel access road again, turning right along it.

Shortly before a right-hand bend in the road, turn right on to a path signposted 'Duchesses Bridal Path'. This is one of a number of lovely old paths on the estate, laid out at a time when drives and viewpoints were created as much to impress visitors as for the pleasure of the owner, the Duke of Atholl. The path stays level for a considerable time, contouring round the hill which falls away very steeply to the left down to the river. The path passes a seat and goes through rhododendron bushes, before making a big swing to the right. At this point the first tall old larches appear on either side. You are likely to see red squirrels in this area, which offers them a plentiful supply of food.

The path becomes broader and climbs to another waymarker. Continue with the broad path until it meets a track crossing your path, and then turn left to reach the edge of a field. Follow the track round several curves almost to the lodge beside the road. Across the road at this point is Polney Loch and to the left is the King's Pass. This was the A9 before the bypass was made.

St Colme's Well.

Turn left just before the lodge on a surfaced track, and after 200m go right on a path through a gate. In a further 300m turn right along a smaller path signposted to St Colme's Well, which is reached in 150m. The well is an attractive stone-arched spring with clear water bubbling out of it. The name Colm(e), otherwise Colman, Colum or Columba, is borne by over 200 saints, believe it or not, and there are many places in both Scotland and Ireland thought to have holy connections named after one or other of these saints. There is a St Colman's Well at Fowlis, near Crieff. Bathing in or drinking from these wells was supposed to effect cures from all manner of ills.

Return to the main path and turn right, immediately going right again, following the signpost for King's

Seat, another very popular placename not always having a connection with any known king! The path emerges from the trees to give a superb view across the hotel buildings to the river and Birnam Hill – certainly a view fit for a king.

Turn at this point and retrace your steps all the way back past the lodge and down through the wood along the Duchesses Bridal Path, round the hill and back down to the hotel driveway. Turn right along the drive and 100 m past the end of the field, turn sharply left (signposted Parent Larch, Bishop's Walk, Cathedral) and enjoy the lovely broad path through the trees with the river just below to your right.

Dunkeld House Hotel, the Tay and Birnam Hill.

Follow the path by the field edge to the left then right, left again over Bishop's Hill, back to the field and right again to meet the cathedral fence. The 'Parent Larch' is just on the left here. The first successful planting of larches in this area was from seedlings brought back from the Tyrol, in Austria, by Colonel Menzies of Glen Lyon. He gave some of them to the 2nd Duke of Atholl, and five were planted here in 1738. Four have gone and this is the only survivor – a venerable tree indeed, which has seen a tremendous parade of Scottish history during its two and a half centuries of life.

Turn left and then right to walk along a path at the field edge. You can then either go left to walk back round Stanley Hill, or right towards the cathedral gates, into Cathedral Street and back through the town to the car park.

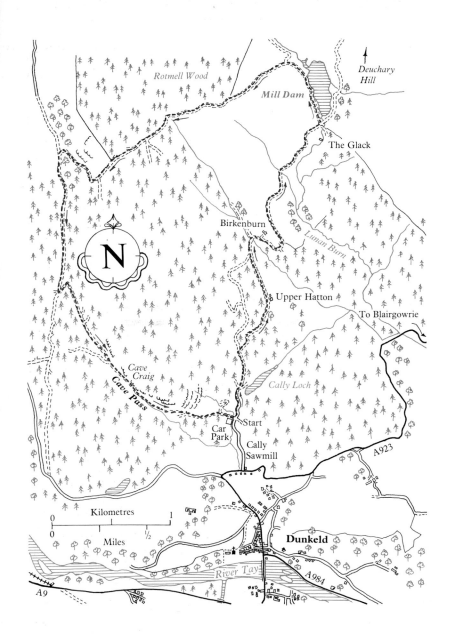

Rotmell Wood

Mill Dam

Deuchary Hill

The Glack

N

Birkenburn

Lunan Burn

Upper Hatton

To Blairgowrie

Cally Loch

Cave Craig

Cave Pass

A923

Start

Car Park

Cally Sawmill

Kilometres

0   1

0   ½

Miles

Dunkeld

A984

River Tay

A9

MILL DAM AND CAVE PASS

This is another very varied walk with good views and a most intriguing little pass near its end. From the car park, return to the track which you drove up and turn left. You may have noticed at the lodge that the track is signposted as a public footpath to Kirkmichael, 24 km (15 miles) away. You are not going that far! The track is also signposted to a house called The Glack, and for the first part of the walk, all that is needed in routefinding is to keep following signs to The Glack.

The track climbs gently through mature woodland on the Atholl Estates. This is a working wood, and you can often hear the sawmill away to the left busy converting raw trunks and boughs into cut logs. A kilometre after leaving the road, Cally Loch is passed, almost hidden in the trees down to the right. The high crags away to the left are a feature of the latter stages of this walk. Continue with the track as it winds up and round to reach Upper Hatton, a beautifully modernised house. In the fields, cattle and horses graze, and just beyond the house, to the right, you will often see fallow deer, which share the grazing with

INFORMATION

Distance: 10 km (6 miles).

Start and finish: The 'Blue Gates' car park. From Dunkeld, take the A923 Blairgowrie road and in 400 m turn left at the lodge on a track. Go up the track for 400 m and the car park is on the left. Despite the name, there are no blue gates!

Terrain: Road, tracks and paths. Parts of the walk can be muddy so strong footwear is advised.

Refreshments: Wide choice in Dunkeld.

Toilets: At car park in Dunkeld.

The track leading up to Mill Dam.

livestock. In the autumn this is an excellent place to watch the bucks rutting.

The track twists right to pass below Birkenburn, crossing a burn by a fine old stone bridge, then heading left again with the views becoming more open. Deuchary Hill is clear ahead and the roofs of The Glack peep through the trees. The track continues climbing until The Glack is reached, 3km after leaving the road. Pass to the left of the houses to reach Mill Dam, a lovely upland loch. Small boats stored here indicate that the loch is fished for trout. This is a tranquil and very attractive spot with a number of good picnic places along its shore.

Keep left of the loch and just past its northern end, where the main track swings sharply right, go left along a grassy track heading for a gap between

Fishing on Mill Dam.

heathery hills. Go through the gap, the track becoming more stony, to walk beside a forestry plantation, Rotmell Wood, with a fence on your right.

Pass through a gate into the wood, which has a mixture of trees, mainly coniferous. Keep straight on at the next junction then go through another gate and continue, now with the wood to your left. The track descends twoards the Tay Valley with Craigvinean Forest dominating the hill opposite and a fine northward view opening up.

Keep with the track as it swings round several curves, then turn left along the broad track which runs straight across the hill. At the edge of the wood note the superb old 'granny' pine up to the left. Go through a gate and continue on the track, which can be rather muddy after rain. There is a marked contrast between the dense spruce plantation to the right and the much more open pinewood to the left.

Go through another gate by a small kissing gate at its side and in a further 250 m go sharply back up to the left on a path which soon twists back equally sharply to the right and continues, climbing steadily. There are deer in this part of the wood. The path levels out and becomes a little overgrown, but persevere. A fence comes in from the left with crags behind it. Where the path makes a U-turn to the right go left over a ladder stile, with big shattered crags (Cave Craig) to the left. The narrow path leads enticingly forward into the jaws of Cave Pass.

Ducking under branches and clambering over boulders, make your way down the pass with a small burn tinkling along beside you. The atmosphere is magical, especially when sunlight filters down creating constantly shifting patterns of light and shade. You may well see red squirrels here – or was that an elf scurrying across the floor of the wood?

Cross the burn at a rather muddy spot and continue through a grotto of gnarled old trees and huge boulders. The path runs along a shelf below huge crags which are sometimes used for rock climbing. Do not continue along this path, but after viewing the impressive crags return, re-cross the burn and turn left. At three large beech trees go left, nearly to the burn, then follow the path down, scrambling over rocks to cross the burn at a real little grotto with a tiny waterfall. You can just imagine fairies coming here to wash. It is called 'Lady Charlotte's Cave'.

A slightly tricky bit follows. Just past the grotto, go downhill under an old pine tree for 20 m to a clear path below. The path soon becomes more open and gives fine views of Dunkeld and Birnam Hill. Wander along, enjoying the views, until you join another broad path and continue easily, soon reaching the parking area.

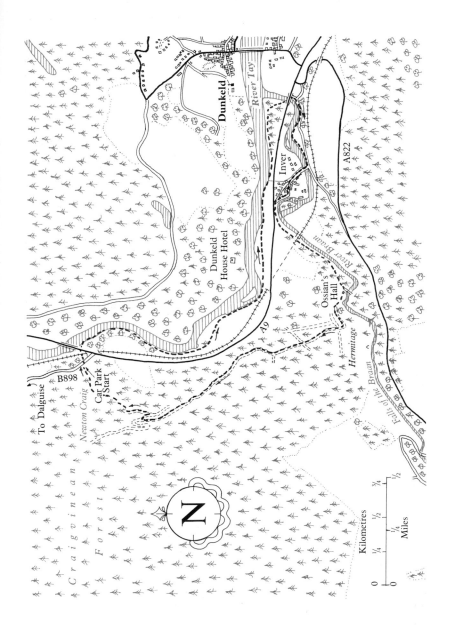

Dunkeld

River Tay

Inver

A822

Dunkeld House Hotel

Ossian's Hall

River Braan

Hermitage

A9

To Dalguise

B898

Newton Crag

Car Park Start

Craigvinean Forest

Falls of the Braan

Kilometres
0   ¼   ½   ¾
0   ¼   ½
Miles

THE BANKS O'TAY

This very varied walk follows the banks of the Tay, visits Ossian's Hall, and passes through part of the large Craigvinean Forest. It provides a fine outing at any time of the year. From the car park, return to the road, cross it and go down the gravel path opposite. It passes under the railway on a 'creep' and then under the A9 bridge, which looks very impressive viewed from this unusual angle. Just to the right of the path here is a British Gas marker which had a bluetit nest inside it in summer 1993!

Continue along the bank of the Tay, a broad river here with both banks well wooded. The path runs along above the river and although the traffic on the A9 is clearly audible it does not spoil the pleasure of the walk. Where the river bends left, climb a short steep bank and continue on an old, very broad path. After 200 m take the left fork and drop down to the river bank again, passing ruined buildings on the right.

INFORMATION

Distance: 8 km (5 miles).

Start and finish: Newton Craig car park, reached by turning off the A9 just south of the bridge over the Tay on to the B898 road (signposted to Dalguise and Grandtully) and then turning left again immediately into the car park.

Terrain: Tracks and paths, some road. Strong footwear advised.

Waymarked: Yes.

Refreshments: Sometimes a van in the Hermitage car park. Otherwise Dunkeld or Birnam.

Opening hours: The Hermitage: Open all year, free.

A glorious show of bluebells.

The riverside path is itself now broad; in midstream is a small shingle island.

At a fork, just past a waterpipe, go left, by the river. You are now opposite the grounds of the impressive Dunkeld House Hotel, with a fine view looking back upriver. Reach a field and cross it, keeping close to the fence on your left. At its far end, with a mound ahead, re-cross the fence and resume the riverside path. Along here is Niel Gow's Tree, an oak named for the great fiddle-player who was born in 1727 at Inver, the village you are now approaching.

The path is narrow and perseverance is required for a short distance but it soon becomes clearer with Dunkeld in view ahead. Cross the Inver mill stream and carry on, the path becoming broad again as it passes through a rather dark plantation. At a junction, turn 90° right to pass below power lines and then through another small wood.

The road bridge over the Tay.

Pass under the A9 again and cross the River Braan by a fine new footbridge. Once over the river, which is less turbulent here than further upstream, turn sharp right along a tarmac path and in 100 m go right again on a minor road (there is a pavement). Walk along beside the river and then Inver Mill caravan park with its thick hedge.

Turn right over a lovely old bridge spanning the Braan, into the neat village of Inver with Forest Enterprise offices and workshops on the right. At the end of the road, turn left and walk beside the A9 for 200 m before turning left and down a slope into The Hermitage car park.

Follow the main path from the car park beside the river, noting the many fine specimen trees. They include both Douglas and Silver Firs. The former tree is named after David Douglas, a noted botanist who discovered many new species and sent the first seeds of this fir back from North America in 1828. These trees were planted in 1919: in their native America they can grow to over 100 m high.

The Hermitage area was presented to the National Trust for Scotland in 1944 by Katharine, Duchess of Atholl, whose husband, the 8th Duke, was the Trust's

Looking back up the Tay.

first president. The track leads to Ossian's Hall, a folly built in 1758 overlooking the Falls of the Braan, a series of rocksteps over which the river crashes impressively (see walk 12 for full details). On the way you can see (post 5) one of the tallest trees in Britain, a Douglas fir well over 65 m high.

When you leave the Hall, go forward for 50 m then turn left along a broad track. After 250 m the track swings right and crosses another track. Go straight over on a forest road (cycleway signs).

After 250 m pass a small informal car park and continue through a gate. The road winds through Craigvinean Forest on a fairly level contour with a steep rocky slope to your left. In 1 km turn very sharply right down another forest road and in 50 m turn sharp left on to a grassy path.

This path leads down through mixed woodland to a small side valley which it follows to the right, descending fairly steeply to reach a forest road. Turn right for a few metres to the car park where you started.

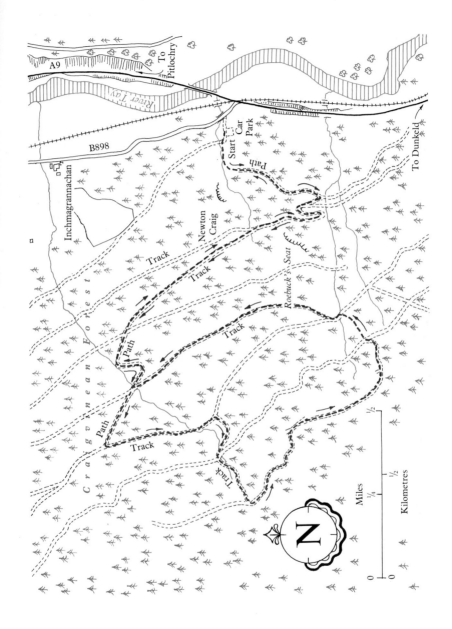

To Pitlochry

A9

River Tay

B898

Start Car Park

Path

To Dunkeld

Inchmagrannachan

Newton Craig

Roebuck's Seat

Track

Track

Track

Craigvinean Forest

Path

Path

Track

Track

N

Miles

¼ ½

0

Kilometres

½

0

CRAIGVINEAN FOREST

This walk provides the opportunity to see a considerable part of Craigvinean Forest at both lower and upper levels. Craigvinean is a large feature in the landscape, and Forest Enterprise has produced an ambitious 25-year programme of thinning, felling and restocking to provide a greater variety of trees of various ages, while retaining some open spaces. It is fascinating to walk through the forest now and try to imagine what it will be like a generation ahead. A display showing what is planned for Craigvinean can be seen at the Queen's View Visitor Centre.

INFORMATION

Distance: 7 km (4 miles).

Start and finish: Newton Craig car park.

Terrain: Forest tracks and paths. Strong footwear advised.

Refreshments: None en route. Nearest at Dunkeld.

Craigvinean Forest and the A9 bridge.

Mountain biking on a forest road.

From the car park, retrace in reverse the last part of walk 16, up beside the burn and then on the footpath which climbs to meet a forest road. Turn right on to the road and carry on uphill, twisting round a sharp double bend. You will see signs indicating that this is a designated route for mountain bikes. If you meet bikers, stand aside for a few seconds to let them pass: they will be travelling more quickly than you, and you should be in no hurry.

As the road straightens out after the double bend, the hillslope above to the left has the charming name of Roebuck's Seat. There are roe deer in the forest, but they are shy creatures and you will be lucky to catch a glimpse of one.

The road climbs steadily. At the fork go left along a track which you follow in a long, steady climb for 1 km. The view back opens up nicely at several points, providing an opportunity for a pause. At the next junction, cross and continue ahead, still climbing but now on a path – tough going for bikes, this one!

The path curves left with an attractive burn tumbling down on the right, then swings back right, still climbing, to meet a track. Turn right, cross the burn and after 20 m go left up another path, climbing more gently for about 250 m to meet a track. Turn left along this broad track, which follows the contours and provides easy walking. Note the area of fine old birch trees to the left. The forward programme provides for this type of planting to be extended, particularly beside burns and around rock features. Cross a burn (actually the same one as you saw earlier) and curve left, passing a small shelter used by forestry workers.

At the next junction, turn right (still following blue bike waymarkers); at the following junction in 250 m, swing left with the main track, and at yet another junction turn left along a broad forestry road – the upper road in the forest. The road swings round several curves. When it ends at a large turning circle, go right onto an old track that winds gently downhill, giving a real feeling of isolation and even secrecy with tall trees to either side. This is a place to soak up the atmosphere of the forest to the full, and it is not

A glorious show of woodland flowers.

difficult to understand why trees were such a vitally important part of many ancient cultures. In Scotland, each letter of the Gaelic alphabet has a tree symbol.

The track winds along and down for an enjoyable kilometre and finally swings very sharply left to reach a junction. Do not take either track but go straight ahead, down the hill, picking your way through the birches. There is no path but no matter: it's fun to weave through the trees, taking your time to find the best line. You should hear a burn away to your left. Head on a tangent towards it and you will soon see a broad track below. You should emerge on this track near to where it crosses the burn.

Turn left, and immediately after crossing the burn, fork right. Follow this clear track for 1 km as it curves round through the forest until you meet the path with the bike waymarkers – on the right this time. Turn along it and retrace your outward route from here back to the car park.

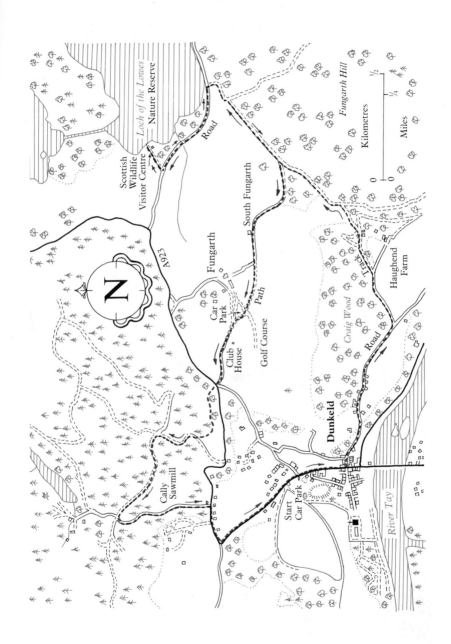

FUNGARTH AND LOCH OF THE LOWES

This walk rises to give excellent views before crossing farmland and passing through woods to return. An optional spur leads to the Scottish Wildlife Trust reserve at Loch of the Lowes. Leave the car park and turn right along the main street (see walk 14 for details). Turn left up Brae Street which rises very steeply, passing the Dunkeld Gallery and Springwells Smokehouse, where you can buy delicious smoked salmon and other fine foods.

Continue up the steep brae which levels out in time, to your relief. After the houses end, the road becomes a narrow lane with little traffic. Pass a layby and a seat on the left and at the sign for Haughend, turn left along a track. Pass the entrance to Haughend Farm, beautifully set below a wooded slope, and continue uphill on the track through mature mixed woodland.

INFORMATION

Distance: 8 km (5 miles). 10 km (6 miles) if spur is added.

Start and finish: The main car park in Dunkeld.

Terrain: Roads, tracks and paths. Some sections can be muddy after wet weather, in which case strong footwear is advised.

Waymarked: Yes.

Refreshments: Wide choice in Dunkeld.

Toilets: At car park in Dunkeld.

Loch of the Lowes.

Go through a gate and continue on the track. In a further 200 m, when the track starts to climb steeply, leave it for a path on the left, by the field edge. Follow this until it meets another track at a gate with a lovely view northwards over Fungarth. The track becomes stony and starts to descend. Another track comes in from the left. This is the eventual return route, but to see Loch of the Lowes, continue on a grassy path beside a dyke and then through a gate to meet a track. Turn left and walk down to the road.

Loch of the Lowes in winter.

Loch of the Lowes, which lies ahead, is a Scottish Wildlife Trust reserve which extends for 98 ha and includes the fringe of surrounding woodland. The birdlife here is outstanding. The first Scottish breeding of great crested grebes was recorded here in 1870, and these lovely birds are still regular inhabitants. In winter the loch holds hundreds of greylag geese, but it is most famous for its breeding ospreys. First seen here in 1969, the 'fish eagles' have returned regularly since then, and breed successfully most years.

There is a small visitor centre with an observation hide at the north-west corner of the loch, which can be reached by going left along the road for about 500 m. It is well worth a visit and with the powerful binoculars provided you have a very good chance of

Osprey.

seeing the ospreys at their nest. There are also many birds in the woodland fringing the loch, including woodpeckers, redstart, goldcrest and flycatcher, and black grouse occur on the surrounding hill slopes.

To continue the walk, return up the track and grassy path to the junction of tracks previously noted and turn right, then swing right and left round bends towards Fungarth. Go through a gate past South Fungarth, and at the next sharp right-hand bend go straight ahead through a gate on a fieldpath. Continue through two more gates and turn left to reach the edge of Dunkeld and Birnam golf course near a shed.

From here, take the track going sharply back and up to the right and follow it to, and then through, the golf club car park and along the access road to the A923. The golf club was founded in 1892 and its notice says that visitors are welcome. Cross the road with great care and go up steps and along a new path towards a dyke with a plantation beyond it. Turn left following the path through an area of fine old beech trees. The path follows the dyke and fence round to the right to join a clear track through the plantation.

At a T-junction 250 m further on, turn left. Go through a gate and into more open woodland, going slightly downhill. At the broad main track, turn left and walk down to the A923. Turn right and follow the road down and then left back into Dunkeld.

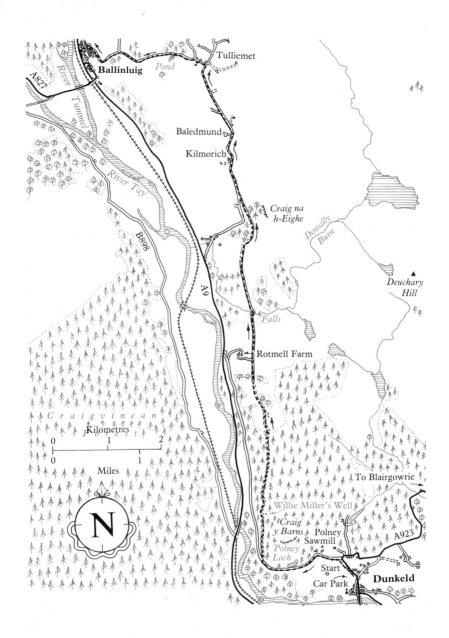

DUNKELD TO BALLINLUIG

This is the longest walk in the book, but it presents no difficulty and offers extremely good views as you progress. It is a 'straight line' walk, with your destination in sight for much of the way, which you may regard as either good or bad according to your point of view!

From the car park in Dunkeld, turn left along the road and at the junction with the Blairgowrie road keep straight on, climbing past Polney Sawmill and a little further on, the peaceful reed-fringed Polney Loch. About 500 m past the loch, leave the road and take the track climbing into the woods on the right.

The track climbs steadily through mixed, mainly coniferous woodland with the crags of Craig y Barns to the right and the busy A9 below to the left. Before long a fine view opens out across the valley to Craigvinean Forest and ahead towards Ballinluig.

INFORMATION

Distance: 14 km (9 miles).

Start: Main car park, Dunkeld.

Finish: Ballinluig. Return by bus – enquire locally for times.

Terrain: Roads and good tracks. Some sections can be muddy. Strong footwear advised, but take your trainers for the road sections.

Refreshments: Ballinluig Inn (open all day).

The Tay and Craigvinean Forest.

After about 1 km of steady climbing, the track levels out. I could find no sign of 'Willie Miller's Well' marked on the 1:25,000 map just right of the track here. Perhaps you will be luckier. At the third junction you join, in reverse, the Mill Dam route (walk 15). Around here a thicker plantation on the left blocks the views for a while.

Above Rotmell.

Leave the woods at a gate and continue along the track (the Mill Dam walk comes down from the right here). You can stride out along the track, which is broad and firm. The views open out again, and at the next gate, there is a particularly fine view of the Tay ahead and Ben Vrackie to the right.

The track stretches ahead, keeping to the same contour. At the cross-tracks above Rotmell Farm, keep straight ahead, now walking between fields of sheep and cattle. Look down to the left and try to imagine the scene in January 1993, when this whole flat area from Ballinluig to Dunkeld was underwater as a result of serious flooding. A number of people in this area had to be rescued by helicopter, but fortunately the flood warning system worked, and no lives either human or animal were lost.

The track dips a little to cross Dowally Burn by a fine old bridge. There are pretty tumbling falls to the right, but for much of the year they are rather hidden by the trees – frustrating for the photographer. The track briefly jinks left and right before resuming its straight-line progress through fields and small woods, often alive with pheasants which crash into the air in their clumsy, clattering way as you startle them.

The track enters a larger plantation with a belt of rhododendrons on the right separating you from open moorland. A clearing gives another splendid view west up the Tay taking in Farragon Hill. On the right here is Creag na h-Eighe – 'the file crag', perhaps named from its sharp edges. The track, often rather muddy in this section, goes gently downhill and reaches the road. Turn right here. At the next gateway on the right there is a natural stone seat where you can perhaps take the opportunity to switch from boots to trainers, the rest of the walk being on roads.

A shaded section of the track.

Walk past Kilmorich, possibly named for Muireadhach, one of the myriad Celtic saints (he died in 1011AD), and then Baledmund, which has the same name as the estate containing Ben Vrackie. Bal or baile is a steading, so this Edmund may have had two farms not far apart, each taking his name. Walk on to Tulliemet, where the road takes a sharp left-hand bend.

From here on it is steadily downhill, passing a fine beech wood on the right and an attractive pond on the left, before the road makes a double bend to reach the village of Ballinluig. Its name may mean 'steading of the bright stream', a reference either to the Tummel or perhaps even the wee burn you saw on the way down the hill. The inn is on your left, in the main street.

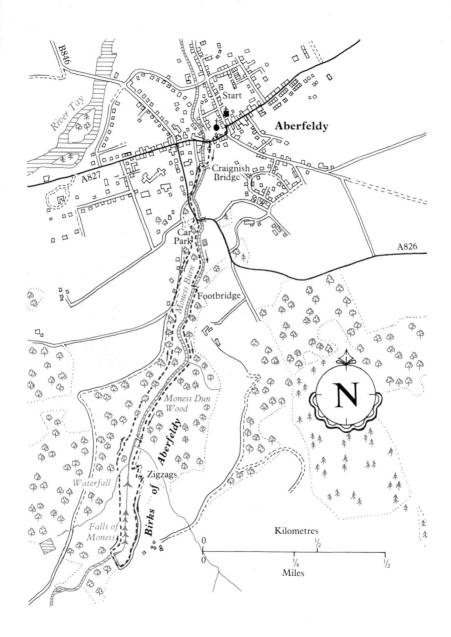

THE BIRKS OF ABERFELDY

The Birks is a popular walk with both locals and visitors, due both to the fine scenery and to the association with Scotland's national poet. Robert Burns is famous as a writer, but here we can consider him as an early conservationist too. He visited Aberfeldy in August 1787, took this walk, and wrote a song to mark the occasion. The fame of the Birks spread and the wooded glen of the Moness Burn has been carefully preserved ever since.

The walk starts in The Square in Aberfeldy, which has a fine ornamental fountain 'erected by Gavin, Marquis of Breadalbane, as a memento of the cordial reception accorded to him and Lady Breadalbane on their first visit after the restoration of the Marquisate, July 1885'. Walk west along the main street for a short distance and then turn left, following the blue sign to the Birks, to pass under the arch of the War Memorial, by neat Birks Cottage and along the path to reach and cross the Moness Burn at Craignish Bridge, originally erected as a plaque records 'through the generosity of Miss Jessica Campbell of Ericht House, Aberfeldy, July 1914'. The bridge was rebuilt in 1990.

Continue on the path beside the chuckling burn; in summer it is a lovely scene of dappled light and shade as the sun strikes through the trees, many of which are indeed birches. 'Birks' is a Scots word meaning either a

INFORMATION

Distance: 6 km (4 miles).

Start and finish: The Square, Aberfeldy. Car parking nearby.

Terrain: Good paths. Some steep climbing. The paths can be muddy after rain, and in such conditions strong footwear is advised.

Waymarked: Yes.

Refreshments: Wide choice in Aberfeldy.

Toilets: In Aberfeldy.

Falls of Moness.

single tree or a birchwood. The path crosses a lade (a man-made water channel, which feeds the working corn mill in Aberfeldy) and then goes up steps – the first of many you will encounter on this walk – to run beside the Crieff Road and then meet it at a gate. Cross with care and walk up the track to a car park, passing some fine specimen trees. You can start the walk from here but I find it more satisfying to do the full trip from the town centre.

An information board describes the Birks and gives the words of Burns' famous song:

> Bonnie lassie, will ye go
> Will ye go, will ye go
> Bonnie lassie, will ye go
> To the Birks of Aberfeldy?
>
> Now simmer blinks on flowery braes
> And o'er the crystal streamlet plays
> Come let us spread the lightsome days
> In the Birks of Aberfeldy
>
> While o'er their heads the hazels hing
> The little birdies blithely sing
> Or lightly flit on wanton wing
> In the Birks of Aberfeldy
>
> The braes ascend like lofty wa's
> The foaming stream deep-roaring fa's
> O'erhung wi' frequent spreading shaws
> The Birks of Aberfeldy

You can assess for yourself the accuracy of the poet's description as you continue the walk past a fine Japanese Cedar. Where the path divides go left, following the sign to the Moness Falls. Moness means 'the foot of the falls', and straightaway you cross a bridge below a small fall. The path climbs a little then drops down to pass beside the burn, which here runs over smooth, water-worn rock.

The path starts to climb in earnest, and for a time is fenced on the right. Small bridges take you over minor burns feeding into the main stream. It is easy to slip into a reverie along here and imagine yourself back in Burns' time, wandering through the 'spreading shaws' (a shaw is a small wood). It seems as though little has changed – until the modern world intrudes in the form of a jet passing overhead!

Continue following the path. The glen is becoming much more gorge-like, with sheer crags on the opposite bank. The path climbs a steep flight of wooden steps and crosses a bridge with a crag to the left. More steps lead to Burns' Seat, where the poet is said to have rested and gained the inspiration for his song. Perhaps if you sit here you too will be blessed with inspiration: the surroundings certainly encourage poetic thought.

Yet more steps, stone this time, lead up beside a fine waterslide and then back to cross the burn above the slide, still with falls on the left. Cross a long wooden bridge; the steep slope opposite has fine trees and a number of dead ones as well. The path leads down to a viewing platform for the Moness Falls, a very impressive sight as the burn tumbles down between high crags.

Side fall, off Moness Burn.

There is still a fair amount of climbing to be done. Return to the main path and continue upward on more steps. The path turns back right and continues zigzagging upward for some time to reach a point with a fine view of the upper falls – and the bridge that crosses them. The path curves right and gives a great view right back down the gorge to distant hills, then continues to the bridge over the falls. Below your feet the water leaps, and as Burns says, 'deep-roaring falls' over the lip.

After one last short climb the long descent begins. Partway down there is a superb view of Ben Vrackie. The return path is perhaps of less interest than the outward route but it is still very pleasant to wander along through the lovely birches, back to the car park. Here you can enjoy the intriguing Tree Trail which takes you in rapid succession past a host of unusual trees including Kashmiri Whitebeam, Antarctic Beech, Young's Weeping Birch, the Angelica or Devil's Walking Stick and a Chinese Scarlet Rowan before you re-cross the road and walk back down to the town centre.

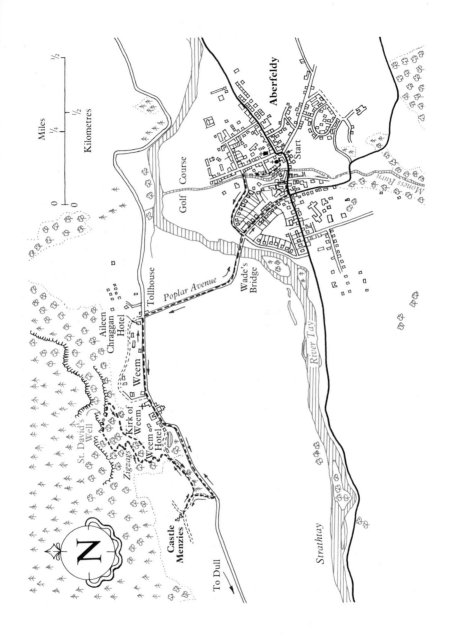

ABERFELDY AND CASTLE MENZIES

Aberfeldy is a bonny town with a long history, and exploring it on foot is well worth doing. This walk extends out from the town to the village of Weem and Castle Menzies. It is of course perfectly possible to drive to the castle, but it is very satisfying to arrive on foot.

From the tourist information centre in The Square, walk past the toilets and down Burnside, noting as you do so that the foundation of the church which now houses the TIC was laid on 28 August 1877 by the Hon. Arthur Kinnaird, MP, and the Rev. John Kennedy, DD, two fine local worthies. At the road junction, turn left over the Moness Burn and then cross the road to go right, down steps into a very pleasant park which includes among its attractions a skateboard ramp and an old traction engine. Away to the right is Aberfeldy Golf Course and its striking new footbridge over the Tay.

Cross the park leftward past toilets to rejoin the road and go right. On the right is a cricket field with benches neatly tiered for spectators. Follow the road to a junction, and cross to view the large and imposing Black Watch Monument. Unveiled in November 1887 by the Marquis of Breadalbane, the monument depicts a soldier wearing the old regimental uniform. Its cost of around £500 was raised by public subscription. The Black Watch (Freiceadan Dubh in Gaelic) was first raised in 1667 by clan chiefs on the order of King George II to keep the peace in the Highlands, and takes its name from the dark tartan it wore. The regiment was given the freedom of Aberfeldy in 1970.

From the green below the monument there is a superb view of Wade's Bridge over the Tay. Built as part of the military road between Stirling and Inverness, it was constructed in a single season between spring and autumn 1733 at a cost of £4095 – easily the most expensive single project in the whole military road network and a magnificent achievement for its time. Although the lovely five-span bridge with its four tapering pillars is always associated with General

INFORMATION

Distance: 7 km (4 miles) or 8 km (5 miles) if St David's Well is included.

Start and finish: The Square, Aberfeldy.

Terrain: Roads and good path to well. No special footwear needed.

Refreshments: Wide choice in Aberfeldy. Tearoom at Castle Menzies.

Toilets: In Aberfeldy and at the castle.

Opening Hours
Castle Menzies: Apr–Oct, Mon–Sat 1030–1700. Sun 1400–1700 (tearoom Mon–Sat 1100–1630, Sun 1400–1630).
Aberfeldy Water Mill: Easter–Oct, Mon–Sat 1000–1730, Sun 1200–1730.

Aberfeldy Church.

Wade, it was actually designed by the famous architect William Adam; it is founded on 1200 wooden piles shod with iron.

Wade's Bridge.

Cross the bridge (with care – the footway is very narrow) and note the plaque on the first pillar on the right giving its provenance and stating that Wade laid the first stone on 23 April 1733. During its construction, the old soldier complained that 'the Justices of Peace promised to furnish carriages for materials at the county's expense, but did not perform it'. He also said that '200 artificers and labourers from the army were employed for nearly a whole year'. They did well: after 260 years and innumerable raging floods on the Tay the old bridge is as solid as ever. From it there is a fine view of Upper Strathtay.

Continue along the road. Today it swings right, but the original line as engineered by Wade went straight on. The road is named on some maps as 'Poplar Avenue'; the original trees were felled in the 1960s but the road has recently been replanted by volunteers. When the pavement ends, cross and walk on the right facing the traffic. At the junction (where there was formerly a tollhouse), swing left to pass the Aileen Chraggan Hotel and reach the village of Weem. The name is a phonetic anglicising of the Gaelic *uamh*, meaning 'a cave', and there are indeed caves in the steep wood above.

Weem has two churches. Beside the present building is the Old Kirk of Weem. The building dates from the late 15th century (though it was much altered in the 17th century, as can be seen by the date 1614 on the roof cornerstones), and is dedicated to St Cuthbert, Bishop of Lindisfarne in the 7th century, who it is said lived as a hermit in the woods here. There was a church of some sort in Weem as far back as 1235. In 1839 the Old Kirk was dedicated by Sir Neil Menzies as a mausoleum for his family and clan, and today it contains many fascinating relics including the huge stone Menzies Monument, two ancient stone crosses taken from a long-disused monastery at Dull, and the St Cuthbert's Cross, said to have been erected on the hill by the saint himself. The key to the kirk can be obtained from Clematis Cottage nearby.

Continue past the Weem Hotel, with its portrait of General Wade on the outside wall. He used the building as his base during the construction of the bridge and road in 1733. Continue along the road for 400m (there is now a pavement) to the entry to Castle Menzies and turn right. At the fork go left for the castle or right for the optional extra walk to St David's Well.

If taking this walk, continue through the car park and into the wood. An extraordinary path, frequently stepped, zigzags up, across and even sometimes back *down* the hill until it runs across the foot of a line of huge crags, in one of which is the well ascribed to St David. It is thought nowadays that this should perhaps be *Sir* David (Menzies), who in 1440 renounced the world and took holy orders. Return to the car park and then on to the castle to rejoin the walk.

Weem has been the home of the Menzies family since at least the 14th century. The first castle here was built at that time, burned, replaced in 1488, burned again, and replaced in 1502 by the oldest part of the present castle, which saw substantial additions in the late 16th century, and again in the 18th and 19th centuries. The castle is a fine example of a fortified house. It was inherited by the Clan Menzies Society in 1957 in a dilapidated condition. Since then a great deal of restoration has been carried out and an extensive tour of the older part of the castle is now offered.

Castle Menzies.

The 18th century wing has gone, but the later addition is now being restored. On its ground floor is an excellent tearoom. A full guide and other interesting material is available at the reception desk. Bonnie Prince Charlie stayed in the castle in February 1746 on his way north to the fateful end to his campaign at Culloden; shortly afterwards his eventual conqueror, 'Butcher' Cumberland, was also here.

After visiting the castle, return by the same route through the village and back over Wade's Bridge to Aberfeldy. Go straight on this time, along Taybridge Road, passing the handsome church with its tall steeple. Turn left at the crossroads and left again as signposted to see the watermill, which can be visited. The huge wheel is a very impressive sight when in operation. From the watermill it is a short step back to The Square.

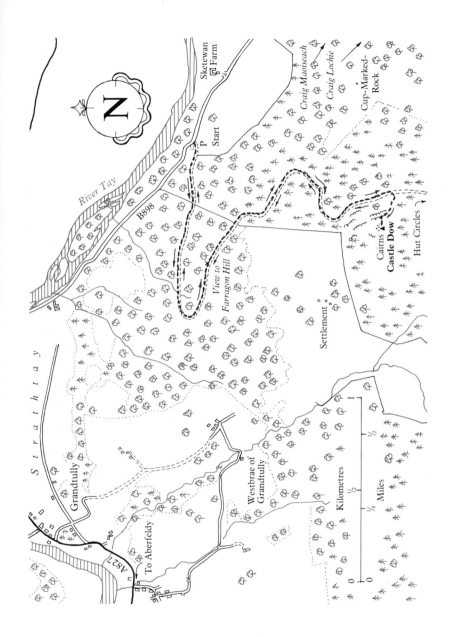

CASTLE DOW

This short walk leads to a most unusual hilltop decorated with 'stone man' cairns which is a magnificent viewpoint, so it is worth saving for a clear day. Go up the track and through a gate. The track climbs steadily through mixed broadleaved woodland with many fine birch and rowan. There are deer in the wood and you may be lucky enough to see them.

After 1 km the track turns sharply back to the left and continues to climb. A particularly good view opens out behind you, with as its central feature Farragon Hill above Aberfeldy with its 'cottage loaf' upper section. Through a gate and before a double bend there is a fine view in the other direction taking in the river and its strath. Continue, noting that the upper part of the wood above you is now a conifer plantation.

INFORMATION

Distance: 6 km (4 miles).

Start and finish: There is no formal parking at the start of this walk, but two or three cars can easily be accommodated. The start is 250 m past the farm of Sketewan, on the B898 road east of Grandtully, where a forest road emerges. The grid reference is 934524. Please be careful not to block the gateway as the forest road is used by timber lorries.

Terrain: Good track, short section of path and open hill. The walk is straightforward and presents no difficulty. No special footwear needed.

Refreshments: None en route. Nearest at Grandtully.

Looking down from the track to Castle Dow.

At the summit of the Castle.

The track bends to the right, with the open moorland of Craig Maoiseach and Craig Lochie over to the left. This whole area is full of ancient field systems, hut circles and signs of settlement dating back thousands of years, which archaeologists are still investigating. You may well see buzzards in this area, and perhaps hear their distinctive mewing cry.

Go through another gate. The bald top of Castle Dow is now clear ahead, with the 'stone men' standing out. Continue along the track round the left side of the hill, still climbing. Where it levels off at an open area, take the clear path going up to the right. Meet and follow a stone dyke for a short distance. At the dyke corner, go right, cross the dyke at a gap and climb inside the dyke to the top of the hill, walking on heather.

The effort of getting here is rewarded both by the

intriguing collection of tall, slender cairns on the summit and by the view. There are about a dozen cairns, but it is not clear whether they are laid out in a pattern. The name Castle Dow probably comes from the Gaelic caisteal dubh, the black castle.

The view is breathtaking. To the west is the distinctive cone of Schiehallion, the 'fairy hill of the Caledonians', and the long line of hills running either side of Glen Lyon. The aspect is marred only by the unsightly scars of mining tracks around Farragon Hill. To the north-east, Ben Vrackie is clear, and below you are the shapely curves of the Tay. It is a place to linger and savour to the full.

The return journey to the car park is made by the same route, enjoying the views in the opposite direction, and also the fact that it is all downhill!

Primroses.

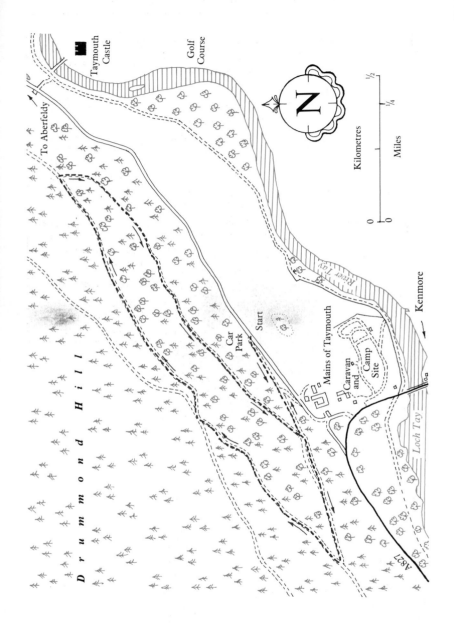

Taymouth Castle

Golf Course

To Aberfeldy

N

Kilometres

Miles

0   1/4   1/2

River Tay

Kenmore

Start

Car Park

Mains of Taymouth

Caravan and Camp Site

Loch Tay

D r u m m o n d   H i l l

A827

DRUMMOND HILL

Drummond Hill was first planted by the lairds of Breadalbane in the 18th century. It was one of the Forestry Commission's first purchases after the Commission was established in 1919 as a response to timber shortages experienced after the ravages of World War One, and has been managed for timber production ever since. The forest now has two walking routes and is also used for orienteering competitions and car rallies on occasion.

INFORMATION

Distance: 6 km (4 miles).

Start and finish: Drummond Hill car park. Turn east off A827 at Kenmore on minor road and after 600 m turn left as signposted. The car park is 200 m up the track.

Terrain: Good forest tracks and paths. No special footwear needed.

Waymarked: Yes.

Refreshments: None en route. Good selection in Kenmore.

Kenmore from Drummond Hill.

From the car park, follow the wide track steadily uphill for 800 m with occasional views of Kenmore and Loch Tay to the left. At a junction, turn sharply right and continue climbing for a further kilometre. The forest contains trees of mixed age and maturity, with a variety of species including Scots pine, Norway and Sitka spruce and Douglas fir. Felling and replanting has taken place throughout the past 80 years and continues today.

Drummond Hill is one of the forests where the capercaillie, Scotland's largest game bird, is found. After becoming extinct in Britain in the late 18th century due to over-hunting and forest clearance, the bird was reintroduced here in 1837. It is often heard before it is seen as it crashes noisily through the forest understorey.

At the next junction, turn left (waymarked for the viewpoint) and continue along another track climbing slightly for 1km before levelling out and then curving right along a short path off the track to the viewpoint. From here you look down on Loch Tay and Kenmore and across the loch to the hills on its south side. From Kenmore, the River Tay, which has the largest catchment area of any river in Britain at nearly 5000 km², starts its journey towards the sea at Dundee. The Tay regularly floods and in January 1993 it and its sister rivers caused extensive flooding over a very wide area from Aberfeldy to Perth. During that flood, the peak flow of over 2200 cubic metres per second (equivalent to half a million gallons of water *every second*) recorded near Perth was the greatest ever recorded in Britain.

From the viewpoint, return to the track junction and take the right fork with the waymarkers. At a bend, a seat gives a further view of the Tay Valley looking towards Aberfeldy, and you can also see Taymouth Castle and its golf course. The castle, which incorporates an older 16th century building, largely dates from the 19th century, but has been unused for some time. Further on there is a fine view of the Tay as it swings sinuously round a bend, often with foaming white rapids, and a little further on again, a superb

View from Drummond Hill.

view of the whole strath with the river winding through woods and farmland.

At a turning point on the track, 1km after the junction, turn right (look carefully for the waymark) down a small path. Just when you thought you'd finished climbing, it goes up again! It soon levels out and then winds through pleasant mixed woodland often alive with birdsong. There are two or three more short climbs along this stretch. The river and castle can be glimpsed on the left through the trees.

The path levels out and crosses a gully where a wooden rail has been erected as a guard following a substantial landslip, always likely to happen on slopes such as this in periods of heavy rain. Just when you think the path is never going to end, it drops down more sharply to rejoin the main forest track 200 m above the car park – and I bet you didn't see the path turn off on the way up! It is indeed well hidden.

Return to the car park at the end of another enjoyable walk.

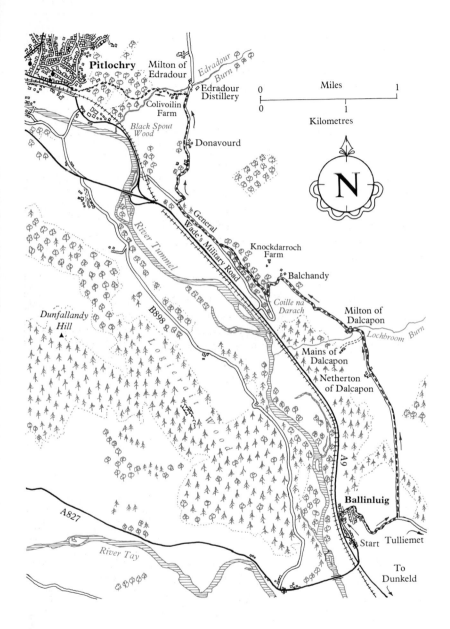

BALLINLUIG TO PITLOCHRY

This route parallels the walk from Logierait to Pitlochry (walk 9), taking the east bank of the Tummel and offering contrasting views as it climbs high above the river. It makes a pleasant, undemanding outing.

Leave Ballinluig by the Tulliemet road which climbs around a double bend. Just past a farm with the intriguing name of Port of Tummel - could this have been a receiving-house for goods brought in by river in times past? - turn left on the Dalcapon road. The road continues to climb steadily, giving fine views across to Logierait Wood and Dunfallandy Hill and northwards towards the Pass of Killiecrankie, with Ben Vrackie prominent to the right.

At its high point, just before Netherton of Dalcapon, there is a super view of the River Tummel and the town of Pitlochry, the colourings especially fine in autumn. Netherton of Dalcapon is passed and then Mains of Dalcapon, two names indicating the standing of these farms when they were established.

INFORMATION

Distance: 8 km (5 miles)

Start: Ballinluig, reached by bus from Pitlochry. Enquire locally for times.

Finish: Pitlochry.

Terrain: Roads and small section on good paths. No special footwear needed.

Refreshments: Ballinluig Inn at start. Pitlochry Pottery en route. Wide choice in Pitlochry.

Opening hours: Edradour Distillery is open Mar-Oct, 0930–1700.

Looking north from near Ballinluig.

Looking across the Tummel
to Logierait Wood.

The road crosses the Lochbroom Burn, which comes down from the loch of its name high on the moors to the east, and wriggles through Milton of Dalcapon, this name indicating the presence of a mill here once. At Balchandy the road swings left and starts to drop. Turn sharp right at the first junction. On the left here is Coille na Darach, meaning 'the oak wood', and the next entry on the right is Knockdarroch Farm, meaning 'oak hill'. There are still some oaks around here, but the trees must have been more plentiful in past centuries.

In 600 m turn right again, at the Pitlochry Pottery and tearoom, which offers refreshments all day and a good range of pottery and other souvenirs. You are now on part of the old military road, engineered by General George Wade in the 1720s. His route from Stirling to Inverness was crucial in keeping communications open for government forces and officers between Lowlands and Highlands, and the modern A9 follows it for a good part of the way between Pitlochry and Dunkeld.

The Tay Valley from above Ballinluig.

At the next junction, you can either press on along the road for a direct way in to Pitlochry or, for a more varied and interesting end to the walk, turn right on the road signposted to Donavourd and Balnald. The road climbs quite steeply, with small woods on its left, to Donavourd, and then continues to climb at a more gradual angle towards Edradour, where the distillery can be visited. Edradour claims to be the smallest distillery in Scotland and the visitor can learn some of the secrets of whisky production and sample the very fine single malt produced here, perhaps taking away a bottle as a reminder of the visit (for full details see walk 7).

To complete the walk, walk through Colivoulin Farm (the name means 'mill wood'), cross the Edradour Burn by the footbridge into Black Spout Wood and follow the paths signposted to Pitlochry. The paths wind through attractive mixed woodland with many fine old trees before returning you to the town centre.

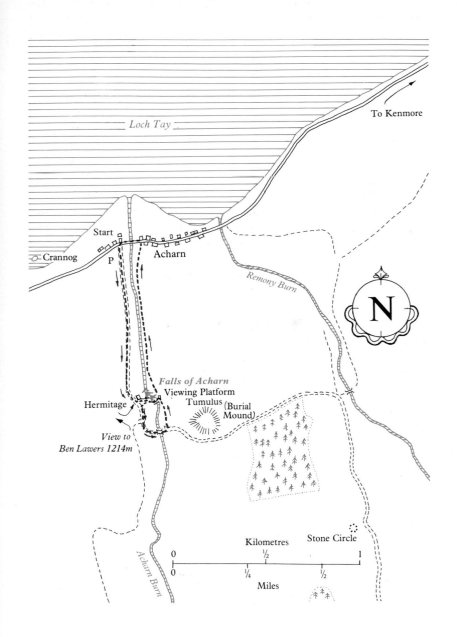

Loch Tay

To Kenmore

Start

Crannog

P

Acharn

Remony Burn

N

Falls of Acharn
Viewing Platform
Tumulus (Burial
Mound)

Hermitage

*View to
Ben Lawers 1214m*

Stone Circle

Acharn Burn

Kilometres
0   ½   1
0   ¼   ½
Miles

THE FALLS OF ACHARN

This is one of the most delightful short walks to be found anywhere, and is ideal for a summer evening or a fine day when you have a couple of hours to spare. To reach the start, drive along the minor road on the south side of Loch Tay from Kenmore and on reaching Acharn cross a neat stone bridge and park tidily on the verge opposite the garage. A sign points up the track towards the falls.

Follow the track, climbing steadily past a farm and two houses; the first often advertises honey for sale and the second houses a registrar of births, deaths and marriages – or as they have alternatively been called, hatches, matches and despatches! This track is occasionally used by large agricultural vehicles extracting timber so be prepared to give way if one comes up or down.

INFORMATION

Distance: 4 km (2 ½ miles).

Start and finish: Acharn village, 3 km west of Kenmore.

Terrain: Good tracks and paths. No special footwear needed.

Waymarked: Yes.

Refreshments: None en route. Good choice in Kenmore.

The Falls of Acharn.

After the initial climb, the track levels off, giving a fine view back over Loch Tay to the forested Drummond Hill (walk 23). The Acharn Burn can be heard rushing down on your left. Opposite a fieldgate, a few paces to the left will bring into view the Hermitage, a viewing chamber for the lower falls set into this side of the gorge. Inside the chamber there is a fireplace and seats; at the time of writing access was difficult, but the chamber can be viewed from the outside and gives a first glimpse of the falls.

Another fine view of the Falls.

Continue a little further along the track, climbing again, until, round a double bend, a sign points left down a path to a viewing platform. The platform and footbridge were built by 202 Field Squadron RE in June 1989 and give a superb view of the Falls of Acharn. To the right, the water thunders down over three rock lips, leaping and crashing from one to another, and then swirls down a long waterslide over the rock beneath the bridge before tumbling sideways over another rock lip to the lower falls below. It is a very impressive place, especially after a period of rain when the falls are well fed with water.

When you are ready to continue, return to the track and continue upwards for a short way to cross the burn by a fine old stone bridge. From here you can enjoy the view along the loch in both directions, and to the grand hills on either side, which include Ben Lawers, at 1214m (3986ft) the highest hill in Perthshire. It is part of a national nature reserve and is owned by the National Trust for Scotland.

When you have enjoyed the view to the full, turn left through a gate on to a path, which leads to another very fine view of the falls from under spreading beech trees – a lovely spot to tarry a while on a fine day.

Continue downhill on the path, passing the footbridge and viewing platform (if you can – another look is very tempting); a little further on a seat gives a grand view across to the Hermitage. The burn has now crashed over the long lower fall and is a considerable distance below in its gorge.

Continue down beside a stone dyke and then a fence, dropping steadily towards the village. Past a small hut containing a hydro-electric plant run by the estate, the path becomes a clear track leading easily down past two more stone water department buildings. Reach the tarmac and walk through an attractive group of houses to the road. Turn left over the bridge for a few metres back to the start of the walk.

Acharn is another place with Rob Roy MacGregor connections. During the 1716–18 period, when he was a hunted man following the failure of the 1715 Jacobite Rising, which he strongly supported, some of Rob's children stayed in Acharn and went to school here. He had relatives at Taymouth and the children were sent here to be safe. Rob's own homes, first in Glen Dochart and then on Loch Lomondside, were burnt by government forces during this troubled period.

INDEX

Other titles in this series

25 Walks – Deeside
25 Walks – The Trossachs

Other titles in preparation

25 Walks – Fife
25 Walks – Galloway
25 Walks – The Border Hills
25 Walks – In and Around Edinburgh
25 Walks – In and Around Glasgow

Long distance guides published by HMSO

The West Highland Way – Official Guide
The Southern Upland Way – Official Guide

HMSO publications are available from:

HMSO Bookshops
71 Lothian Road, Edinburgh, EH3 9AZ
031-228 4181 Fax 031-229 2734
49 High Holborn, London, WC1V 6HB
071-873 0011 Fax 071-873 8200 (counter service only)
258 Broad Street, Birmingham, B1 2HE
021-643 3740 Fax 021-643 6510
33 Wine Street, Bristol, BS1 2BQ
0272 264306 Fax 0272 294515
9-21 Princess Street, Manchester, M60 8AS
061-834 7201 Fax 061-833 0634
16 Arthur Street, Belfast, BT1 4GD
0232 238451 Fax 0232 235401

HMSO Publications Centre
(Mail, fax and telephone orders only)
PO Box 276, London, SW8 5DT
Telephone orders 071-873 9090
General enquiries 071-873 0011
(queuing system in operation for both numbers)
Fax orders 071-873 8200

HMSO's Accredited Agents
(see Yellow Pages)

and through good booksellers

Printed in Scotland for HMSO by CC No. 45489 50C 4/94